DETAIL PROCESS CHARTING

SPEAKING THE LANGUAGE OF PROCESS

BEN B. GRAHAM

WILEY

JOHN WILEY & SONS, INC.

Published by John Wiley & Sons, Inc., Hoboken, New Jersey.

Published simultaneously in Canada

For general information on our other products and services, or technical support, please contact our Customer Care Department within the United States at 800-762-2974, outside the United States at 317-572-3993 or fax 317-572-4002.

Wiley also publishes its books in a variety of electronic formats. Some content that appears in print may not be available in electronic books.

For more information about Wiley products, visit our Web site at *www.wiley.com*.

Library of Congress Cataloging-in-Publication Data:

Graham, Ben B.
    Detail process charting : speaking the language of process / Ben B. Graham.
        p. cm.
        Includes index.
        ISBN 0-471-65394-2 (cloth)
        1. Industrial organization--Charts, diagrams, etc. 2. Organization charts. 3. Reengineering (Management) 4. Benchmarking (Management) 5. Organizational effectiveness. I. Title.
        HD38.153.G73 2004
        658.4'02--dc22

                                                    2004001725

Printed in the United States of America

10 9 8 7 6 5 4 3 2 1

For Tiffany, Ben, Andy, John, Emily,
Mom, and Dad

CONTENTS

LIST OF EXHIBITS

FOREWORD

During the twentieth century, the United States became the most productive nation in the world. This, in turn, has given us a standard of living that makes us the envy of most of the world. Many factors have combined to generate this prosperity. One of these factors, which has contributed trillions of dollars to our benefit, works behind the scenes unknown to the population that enjoys these benefits. This factor is *work improvement tools*—tools designed to enable people to study and improve the way they do their work.

This book thoroughly describes what, in my estimation, is the one twentieth-century work improvement tool most appropriate for the twenty-first century. It was specifically developed to chart and improve information processing at a time when the people who were actually doing that type of work made up only an insignificant portion of the labor force. The labor force was then made up mostly of blue-collar employees working in factories.

Times have changed! Today, the two largest categories of the U.S. labor force are professional (first) and clerical (second), and their work is made up almost exclusively of information. Most of us are in the information-processing business.

The earliest uses of this detailed information process charting technique were directed at smoothing out paperwork by studying what people did with their forms and records, step by step. This technique focused on information processes at a time when people were rather oblivious to work processes. We have been living in an information society for close to a quarter of a century, and the general public still knows little and cares less about information processes—except when they find themselves inconvenienced and frustrated by the bureaucratic nonsense that so often permeates the processes. But behind the scenes, a lot of people have become aware of processes, and consider them to be the most important factor in work improvement.

The fact that so much bureaucratic nonsense still exists is indicative of where we stand in the development of the information society. Wherever we have people making excuses for their work (e.g., "I'm sorry but that's our procedure. We have to do it that way. I know it doesn't make sense."), we have another example of people locked into processes rather than being the masters of them. In spite of all the brilliant technology at our disposal, we are still in the early stages of the Information Age, as we were before mechanical drawing and interchangeable parts in the Industrial Age.

Sure, the word is out that processes are important. But, unfortunately, a lot of the work that is being done improving processes has lacked the rigor needed to do it well. Sometimes people attempt to chart processes by using flowcharts designed for computer systems work, but these are unable to follow the individual records and do not show the steps of work that the people do. Sometimes the charting has been little more than sketches of boxes and lines created from a conversational walk-through of a process. Sometimes there has been no charting at all. Yet, regardless of the approach, in time, improvements have usually been found because there is so much room for improvement.

Because these improvement efforts seem disorganized, they do little for the confidence of the people performing them, and they discourage the thought of continuous improvement. But these efforts could have produced finer improvements much more quickly with less effort and cost if rigorous technique had been used. And, they could have resulted in building libraries of process charts maintained on computers providing the fundamental ingredients needed for continuous process improvement. Here, now, is a book that makes this rigorous technique available.

This technique was, from its inception, intended for use with teams of experienced employees. That is not a new idea. Involving employees in improvement was being done by a lot of the best companies in the mid-twentieth century. (A number of these companies were singled out as world leaders by Tom Peters and Bob Waterman in their book *In Search of Excellence* in 1983.) These companies were using a technique called *work simplification*. From its beginning in the 1930s, work simplification focused on making use of the first-hand experience of the people who did the work. But work simplification was being done in the factories, and usually involved only one person. They didn't require teams.

Improving information processes calls for interdepartmental teams of employees in order to capture the first-hand experience of the different parts of the process. This rubs against the grain in a lot of organizations. I can remember managers looking at me as if I was daft when I suggested that members of different departments work together on teams. On one occasion, the reaction was, "Departments working together on projects! That will never happen in this organization." In a different company I was told, "I can see how it would work here, but our managers aren't ready for that." Today the reaction to employee teams is generally one of acceptance. In some organizations, teams have become commonplace—even interdepartmental teams.

One of the major catalysts in bringing about this change was M. Scott Myers, a consultant with whom I worked. His book *Every Employee a Manager* (McGraw-Hill, 1991) introduced the notion of *functional silos*. This concept has helped a lot of people to see the need for getting past the barriers to interdepartmental cooperation.

So, here we are at the start of a new millennium, trying to get our hands around the work of an information society, absolutely loaded with exciting new technology. We have companies being led by people who are aware of the crucial importance of process improvement and who are also amenable to the idea of having their employees involved in those improvement efforts.

This book explains the detailed process charting technique carefully enough that a person with reasonably good graphic skills can expect to be able to use the technique after reading it. So, get started. Build a library of process charts, and you will find that the obvious improvements they reveal will much more than cover the cost of the effort. Keep track of the savings, chart by chart. Your investment of time and effort will more than pay for itself. And, you will have a fine library of process charts (available at no cost) for training, for continuous improvement, to satisfy regulatory and/or certification requirements, to raise to a professional level the process analysis you are doing with Six Sigma, business process reengineering, and so on, and to put the people of your organization firmly in control of—make them the masters of—their processes.

DR. BEN S. GRAHAM JR.

PREFACE

Any process, however convoluted, disorganized, and complicated, can be broken down and interpreted with a process chart. The method for accomplishing this isn't new. In fact, the method has been producing outstanding results with manufacturing processes for nearly a century and with information processes for more than 50 years!

This book is written for people in all levels in all organizations who wish to gain stronger control of their work environment. It revisits the work simplification approach to process improvement that dominated the work improvement arena for a good part of the twentieth century, with particular attention to the principal tool for information process improvement—the detail process chart. The method described in these pages offers the reader a trained set of eyes, a different (not new) way to look at work.

It is not intended that the methods of work simplification be applied by individuals at their workstations, but rather by workgroups, teams of people involved in different parts of the work processes working together to improve the work they share. In fact, the more people that get involved in work simplification, the more opportunities for improvement will arise. Typically, the more documents change hands, the more opportunities for improvement there will be.

There are many arguments as to who should be involved in improvement work and what kind of solutions to look for—whether to use outside help or internal resources, whether to apply radical solutions or incremental solutions, whether improvement efforts should be top-down or bottom-up. The methodology described in these pages suggests that when these "either–or" arguments force a choice between one option or the other, they are futile. All of those options have their place, and the key is to know when. The work simplification approach first and foremost taps into the process-specific experiences of the people who do the work but also calls upon external resources for technology-specific expertise and alternative perspectives. The process itself determines the potential scope of the solution. Although solutions can be radical, there is no place for a "clean-slate" approach that ignores the current process and the experience of the people who do the work! Finally, it organizes both top-down and bottom-up participation!

The vision must come from the top. Executives must make it clear what they expect to achieve. They must provide direction and show that they are committed. Direction encourages the working people to work together with shared objectives as they apply their best judgment in improving the work that they do. It solidly places the responsibility for the completion and improvement of the work with the people who do it. Commitment comes two ways—with an assurance that there will be no loss of employment as a result of process improvement and with a promise to support the recommendations made by the improvement teams. This doesn't necessarily mean 100 percent acceptance (although upfront approval is a great goal to shoot for as employee teams demonstrate their effectiveness and earn the confidence of management), but it does mean approval of all recommendations that management is not strongly (and validly) opposed to.

Improvements come from the people closest to the work, the ones who live it and breathe it day in and day out—the people who do the work. When the operating people are given the opportunity to participate in an improvement process, their ingenuity is transformed from simply doing the work to improving the way they do it. Benefits include reduced resistance, improved morale, and better solutions! Instead of using creativity to thwart changes that are thrust upon them, they develop creative solutions that they are pleased with and proud to live with.

The methodology presented in these pages is not offered as a panacea. It is simply a powerful, straightforward, proven tool designed specifically for displaying facts about process and taking advantage of the insights that these displays provide. It has been used for more than half a century in organizations large and small, in government and industry. Its roots go back to the earliest tools devoted to the study of information processes (paperwork simplification); it evolved directly from the tools of work simplification that had, by that time, been used and proven in manufacturing for nearly half a century.

ACKNOWLEDGMENTS

First and foremost, to my father, Dr. Ben S. Graham Jr., who introduced me to work simplification and process charting. He has been an exceptional mentor and sounding board throughout my career, and as a result his thoughts and his words are woven into the fabric of this book. He provided exceptional editorial feedback throughout the writing of this book, with significant contributions in the preparation of Chapter 8.

I would like to recognize the contribution of my grandfather, Ben S. Graham Sr., who, while director of methods research for the Standard Register Company in the 1940s, recognized a need to bring improvement tools into the office and in his pursuit of "paperwork simplification" developed the methodology that is the focus of this book.

Thanks also to the process charting experts whose contributions to this book exemplify the value of detail process charts. They include Allen Back, Sharon Cunningham, Merle Laird, Hector Piña, Valerie Rausch, Bill Roach, and Todd Rigby.

1

INTRODUCTION

I didn't understand it much because what the colonel said was full of tactics talk.
Later the captain explained it, and that was better but not much. So then Sergeant
Tyree showed it to us by drawing lines on the ground with a stick. That way it was
clear as could be.

—Shelby Foote

Since the first lines were scratched into the dirt, people have been drawing pictures
to help them explain things. People understand pictures.

There are a number of techniques available for charting (or mapping) business
processes. This book focuses on one of these. The work simplification approach is
at the same time simpler and yet more detailed than most others. It is a method that
has proved itself over and over again during the past century, producing billions of
dollars in process improvement savings. It is a method that can be understood by
anyone at any level in an organization. It is a method that can provide results in a
matter of days—and it is critically needed *today* given the turbulent nature of our
work processes. It is a method that helps us to really *engineer* our work processes.

The study of work as a science, or *scientific management*, really began in the
latter part of the nineteenth century with the work of Frederick Taylor, Frank Gilbreth, and others.[1] Gilbreth, in his search for the "one best way," developed a collection of tools for studying work that later became the foundation of the industrial
engineering discipline. One of these tools was the flow process chart—a lined,
columnar form with sets of five symbols running down the page and a space adjacent to each set of symbols for a brief description. It was this tool that did so much
for manufacturing during the first half of the twentieth century and is the foundation of the charting method described in these pages. This stated, the material presented in this book, while not original, is a new presentation of the work. It
includes the contributions of a few exceptional people who are considered the pioneers in the field of *work simplification* and the concept of *participative manage-*
ment. It is an attempt to state simply how the solid, common-sense approach of
work simplification can help organizations today.

1

Gilbreth understood the basic rules of problem solving—define the problem and break it down. He spent his working life developing tools that help us break down work so that it can be improved. Frank's wife, Lillian, was closely involved in her husband's work, and when he passed away in 1924, she made it her life's pursuit and continued for more than 50 years. She once said, "There is too much study of work that should be eliminated, not studied." It is often the case that the best solution for improving a piece of work is to stop doing it. Good tools help make that decision obvious. The right tools can make a seemingly insurmountable task a quick study. The charting method presented in these pages is one of these tools.

In 1947, American Society of Mechanical Engineers (ASME) did something that was, even then, a long time in the making. It established a set of symbols as the ASME Standard for Operation and Flow Process Charts. Twenty-five years earlier in 1921, Gilbreth had presented "Process Charts—First Steps in Finding the One Best Way" at the ASME Annual Meeting. By the time the symbols were standardized, they had evolved into a solid set of symbols that covered every aspect of work, in any work environment, that can be used with very little confusion. The first process charts appeared as a series of symbols strung down a page in sequential order. This was (and still is) a simple and effective way to track the flow of one item, a person, or a piece of material through a work process.

Exhibit 1.1 shows a breakdown of the basic work elements defined by Gilbreth. Gilbreth originally used a small circle to represent transportation (the wheel of a cart), which has since been replaced by an arrow.

In practice, the operation symbol is filled in when representing a physical change to an object. This way, the *value–added* steps stand out. Gilbreth used this symbol and referred to it as the *Do operation* (see Exhibit 1.2).

OPERATION   TRANSPORTATION   INSPECTION   STORAGE/DELAY

Operation (Doing work). An operation occurs when an object is arranged or prepared for another step, assembled or disassembled or intentionally changed.

Transportation (Moving work). A transportation occurs when an object is moved from one work area to another.

Inspection (Checking work). An inspection occurs when an object is verified for quality or quantity in any of its characteristics.

Storage/Delay (Nothing happening). A storage occurs when an object is kept and protected against unauthorized removal. A delay occurs when an object waits for the next planned action. (A "D" symbol is sometimes used to distinguish a delay from storage.)

EXHIBIT 1.1   BASIC WORK ELEMENTS

DO OPERATION

EXHIBIT 1.2 DO OPERATION

Allan Mogensen studied the Gilbreth methods while pursuing a degree in Industrial Engineering at Cornell University in the 1920s. As a young industrial engineering consultant, Mogensen introduced a concept to the study of work that was to shape his career and earn him the title of the Father of Work Simplification. He realized that improvements that were developed by employees doing the work had the best chance of being successful.

In his book, *Common Sense Applied to Motion and Time Study*,[2] Mogensen addressed and offered solutions for many of the concerns that still snag improvement efforts:

- He offered two primary reasons that people resist change: "First of all, we resist anything that is new; secondly, we all resent criticism."[3]
- He addressed benchmarking and the potential scope of work as follows: "Comparison with similar practices or parts of such practices may offer opportunities for radical revision."[4]
- Regarding continuous improvement, Mogensen wrote, "A chart of the process finally adopted serves as a basis for still further and stimulative improvements. Arrangements should be made for periodical review."[5]
- He even addressed technology for technology's sake: "The process chart enables one to reject the things which are just new—unless they are really better."[6]

In 1932, Mogensen founded *work simplification*, which is defined as the organized application of common sense. He used the process chart (among other tools) to organize and study work, and he drew upon the common sense of the people who did the work for improvement ideas. Mogensen defended participative improvement with these words: "The person doing the job knows far more than anyone else as to the best way of doing that job, and therefore is the one person best fitted to improve it." It is this focus on the human element of work simplification that distinguishes it from other improvement techniques. It is predicated on people who do the work being involved in the work improvement. It does not treat people, products, and information as inputs and outputs, using accounting terminology. It regards people as a treasured resource, the safekeepers of the corporate (or organizational) memory, which is the most vital factor in successful continuous improvement! Mogensen described the process chart as follows:

> In order to achieve measurement, tools are needed and the most important of these is the process chart....Once a process chart has been drawn up, common sense is all that is needed to improve efficiency and better the

process being examined....The process chart then, is the lifeblood of work simplification. It is an irreplaceable tool. It is a guide and stimulant. It takes time to properly utilize but there is absolutely no doubt that it works.[7]

Mogensen began conducting Work Simplification Conferences at Lake Placid in 1937 and continued them for nearly 50 years! (Lillian Gilbreth was part of the original staff, returning each year until the mid-1960s.) Ben S. Graham Sr. (the author's grandfather) was a student at Mogensen's 1944 Conference. He was unique in his class in that he did not come from a manufacturing environment. He learned the methods of work simplification and adapted them from the factory into the office while directing the paperwork simplification effort at The Standard Register Company. There he developed the horizontal process flow chart to accommodate multiple information flows. He also embraced an employee team approach to process improvement that is summarized in this statement made in 1958: "Participation by the worker in developing the method eliminates many causes of resistance and assures enthusiastic acceptance. This is more important than all the techniques put together."[8] He subsequently joined Mogensen's staff as the resident expert in paperwork simplification.

Graham recognized that information processes usually include several documents that are interdependent on each other and that one item can't be isolated and analyzed effectively without considering its effect on the other items, and vice versa. He expanded process charting to show the relationships between multiple items. He also added two variations of the value-added operation symbol that provided particular advantage in information processing (see Exhibit 1.3). The Origination symbol represents when information is first added to a new item introduced into a process. The Add/Alter symbol represents all information changes to an item following its origination. These symbols were incorporated into a revised ASME Standard in the early 1970s. They show value-added steps in information processing.

ORIGINATION   ADD/ALTER

Origination. An origination represents the creation of a record or a set of papers by entering information.

Add/Alter. An add/alter represents an addition or change of information.

EXHIBIT 1.3   VALUE-ADDED SYMBOLS FOR INFORMATION PROCESSING

Graham's contributions earned him recognition as the Founder of Paperwork Simplification. The type of process chart that he developed is often referred to as a *Graham Chart*. The process charting technique presented here is fundamentally the same as the methodology developed by Graham.

WHY SHOULD WE CHART OUR PROCESSES?

The value of information processing is indirect. We process information to satisfy legal requirements and to help people do their jobs better. Why should we chart our processes? Preparing a process chart is not a productive activity, either. The reason that we draw process charts is indirect at a second level. We chart processes to provide information about the work. This information is used to satisfy regulatory or certification requirements, to provide instruction, and to provide a baseline and serve as a tool for improvement. We chart processes to make them better so that they, in turn, can do a better job of helping people do their jobs better.

What is a process? A process is a series of steps that must be completed in order to achieve a particular result. A process chart is a snapshot of a process. In business, processes are the things we do, the activities we perform day to day that keep our organizations going. They are what we do to make, promote, and deliver our products, the things we do to get paid and pay our debts, and the administrative things we do to keep things going, to keep track and to satisfy organizational, regulatory, and legal requirements.

Since a process implies motion, we represent movement (or flow) as a series of steps along a line. The line represents the item being acted upon. The line is followed from one end to the other to see its flow. The symbols on the line represent activities (and periods of nonactivity) that must be completed in order to move forward toward completion. They are placed on the line in the sequence that they are to be completed.

A process chart, then, is a series of symbols along a flow line. Each symbol or step must be completed in order to move forward along the line and complete the process. It is a graphical procedure; it tells the reader what documents, forms, files, and other items are used, where the work is done, in what order it is done, and who does the work

TO HELP PEOPLE DO THEIR JOBS BETTER

There are a number of more specific, more detailed reasons why you might want to chart a process. In each case, the goal is still to understand the process better so that someone can do his or her job better. Process charts answer these questions:

- What is being done?
- By whom? Where? When?

After those questions are answered, we ask, "Why?" to the answers, and better methods become apparent.

Process charts are used for several reasons:

- To identify problems
- To help fix problems
- To assist in the development of new processes
- To compare and standardize similar processes
- For training or educating managers, workers, new people, auditors
- For writing procedures
- To satisfy audit and certification requirements
- To establish a baseline as a foundation for future improvements

Drawing detailed process charts can be quick and easy if you follow the guidelines outlined in this book.

METHODOLOGY OVERVIEW

Drawing process charts is just a part of the work simplification methodology—but an integral part. The process chart is the principal tool for improvement. The chart lays out the job so that it can be reviewed in an organized, structured manner. Process charts break down the job and permit an improvement team to focus its improvement effort on the detail that can be studied step by step. The work simplification improvement approach is organized in a five-step pattern. Drawing process charts fits into the second step—breaking down the process. There are many other tools that may be used for addressing specific issues (facilities layout, Venn diagram, responsibility chart, man-machine chart, etc.), but the process chart is by far the most universally applicable tool in the toolset. Here is the five-step pattern for achieving results with work simplification (also referred to as the *scientific method*):

1. Select a process to study and define the project.
2. Gather the facts. Break it down, prepare a process chart.
3. Challenge the current method, step by step. Question the job and challenge each detail.
4. Develop the improvement. Eliminate, combine, change sequence, simplify.
5. Apply the improvement. Obtain approval, install, measure, follow up.

You will notice a similar pattern with many formulas for improvement. For example, Edwards Deming's PDCA Cycle—Plan, Do, Check, Action—and Six Sigma's DMAIC system—Define, Measure, Analyze, Improve, and Control. The charting method described here may be easily incorporated into these other improvement methodologies.

Chapter 2 outlines the principal roles in a process improvement program. Following chapters address the other steps of the process improvement methodology but with major focus on Step 2—fact gathering and documenting the facts (reality) with a process chart.

ENDNOTES

1. On October 12, 13, and 14, 1911, pioneers in the field of scientific management gathered at Dartmouth College for the first Conference on Scientific Management. Participants included Frederick Taylor, Frank B. Gilbreth, Dr. Lillian M. Gilbreth, Henry L. Gantt, Harrington Emerson, and many others. Taylor and Gantt both had seminal works published in that year: Taylor's *The Principles of Scientific Management* and Gantt's *Work, Wages and Profits*. Emerson's *Efficiency: As a Basis for Operations and Wages* was published in 1909, and Gilbreth's *Field System* and *Bricklaying System* were published in 1908 and 1909 respectively.

2. Allan H. Mogensen, *Common Sense Applied to Motion and Time Study* (McGraw-Hill, 1932).

3. Ibid., 17.

4. Ibid., 39.

5. Ibid., 39.

6. Ibid., 40.

7. Allan H. Mogensen with Rosario "Zip" Rausa, *Mogy: An Autobiography* (Idea Associates, 1989), 44–46.

8. In a letter to his son, Ben S. Graham Jr., June 1958.

2

WHO IS INVOLVED IN PROCESS IMPROVEMENT?

The excellent companies treat the rank and file as the root source of quality and productivity gain.

—Thomas J. Peters and Robert H. Waterman Jr.

Improvement focus may be limited to individuals, workgroups, or departments, or it may become a part of the corporate culture, practiced by everyone in an organization. This chapter addresses the grand-scale approach to improvement where looking for a better way is a part of the job. An ideal process improvement program would involve everyone in an organization. Vision, direction, and commitment come from the top. Improvements come from the people closest to the work. The *continuous improvement program* and, indeed, each individual project are guided by management and carried out in the trenches. A core group of work-improvement experts ties it all together. The specific titles used in this framework are not important—except that they will be used consistently to reflect the roles as defined in this chapter. These roles engage everyone in the organization in process improvement. The roles are organized into the following three groups:

1. Executive Oversight Team
2. Process Improvement Group
3. Process Improvement Projects

EXECUTIVE OVERSIGHT TEAM

The Executive Oversight Team provides vision, support, and encouragement to project teams, makes sure that ideas are heard and addressed, and recognizes people for good results. It doesn't get into the details. It doesn't participate on project teams. It establishes priorities, identifies core processes, enables projects by arranging for funding and manpower, and reviews the effectiveness of the program.

9

PROCESS IMPROVEMENT GROUP

The Process Improvement Group is directed by a *process improvement champion* (the group manager), and consists of *improvement project facilitators* who provide internal consulting services throughout the organization, and a person to manage a *process library*. The facilitators prepare process charts and facilitate improvement teams made up of people who are directly involved in the processes being studied.

Process Improvement Champion

The process improvement champion manages the continuous improvement program. The project facilitators and the process library manager report to this person. This person is an ambassador for continuous improvement and touts the benefits of process improvement and process management, selling the program throughout the organization.

Improvement Project Facilitators

Improvement project facilitators manage improvement projects. They work with client process owners (department, division, function, unit, etc.) to define projects. The facilitator is the process chart and work improvement expert who prepares process charts, explains the charts to process improvement team members, provides charts for the team members to study, and recharts the process to incorporate their new ideas. Facilitators guide the process improvement team (the process experts) through analysis, cost and benefits calculations, proposal preparation, and installation of the improvements.

Process Library Manager

The process library is the foundation for managing continuous process improvement. It is a repository for workflow blueprints—process charts and other process-related documentation. Process charts show how each of the organization's processes works. Collectively, they show how the organization works. The *process library manager* is the gatekeeper for the process library. This person monitors all updates to the library, provides assistance to anyone needing access to the library, and maintains a maintenance schedule for library content—a maintenance review schedule.

PROCESS IMPROVEMENT PROJECTS

A Process Improvement Project is a results-oriented effort to improve the effectiveness of a given work process or group of processes. A successful project requires contributions from management, staff, operating people, and specialists. As a project unfolds, its ownership changes, and with this ownership passes the responsibility to serve as the driving force behind its progress. Management will own the project on two occasions: (1) at its inception to endorse the project, and (2) near the end of the project when management is called on to approve the recommendations of the project team. The project is sponsored by the *process owner* with support from other managers who control parts of the process. The analysis work is conducted by a *process improvement team* that is made up of people involved in the process and is guided by a *process improvement facilitator.*

Process Owner

The process owner is the senior manager who will be the ultimate decision maker for a project. This is the person who approves a project, outlines the project scope, and establishes project objectives. This person's span of control includes all the areas being studied. The process owner formally announces the project and then hands the project off to the project team. At this point, the process owner backs away from the project and allows the team to take control of the work. When the project team presents its proposal for change, the process owner makes the final decision on each recommendation.

Visibly Endorse the Project.   With an announcement to all the areas affected by the project, the process owner formally hands off ownership of the project to the project team. It is important that the process owner and the other managers back away from the project at this time and wait until the team calls a meeting to present its proposals. This promotes a sense of trust and confidence in the team. It also places the responsibility for recommending and making changes to the work squarely where it belongs, with the people who are directly involved with the process.

Approve Recommendations.   At the proposal presentation, the process owner and other managers allow the team members the opportunity to present the entire proposal, uninterrupted. This is usually only a few minutes and consists of reading the recommendations. Following the presentation, the process owner assumes ownership of the project and control of the meeting by taking the following actions:

- Addressing each recommendation one by one, inviting discussion, approval, or rejection
- Approving favorable recommendations and approving those to which the managers are indifferent
- Summarizing the results with a definitive approval or rejection of each recommendation (In some cases, a manager may have reservations about a particular recommendation, without necessarily rejecting it. In this situation, the

process owner assigns that recommendation to the manager who has the reservation and puts it on hold for one week, allowing team members time to rework the recommendation. If the manager still has reservations after this time, it is rejected. In the meantime, the team should have already proceeded with the installation of the approved recommendations.)

- Assigning or approving an installation coordinator and formally announcing the installation to all people who will be affected by it
- Recognizing individual and group contributions

Upon successful installation of the recommendations, the project ends. It will have been a cooperative effort between management, staff, and operating people. The process chart and other process-related documentation will be transferred into the process library, and a follow-up review will be scheduled. The process will be routinely monitored.

Other Managers

There are other managers whose span of control covers a portion of the project, and they have a role in the project as well. These managers typically report to the process owner. Along with the process owner, they endorse the project and review and approve the recommendations. The process owner will look to these other managers for arguments supporting the approval or rejection of recommendations in their areas.

Project Team Members

Project team members represent the different areas through which the process passes and serve as the experts for the steps performed in their areas. Team members are able to understand a process chart and can explain it. They challenge existing methods and offer suggestions for improvement. Team members respect the expert opinions of other team members representing different areas.

Team members look for and accept ideas from outside the team, but the team ultimately decides what it believes is best. Team members perform information-gathering tasks between meetings. They use cost/benefit analysis to support specific recommendations, with a focus on return on investment (what it will cost and what they will get out of it). Then they prepare drafts of new forms and reports to help the decision makers understand the value of the recommended changes.

Project Team Leader

The *project team leader* is usually a respected, veteran employee who works in an area that is central (critical) to the process. The team leader manages administrative tasks and runs the team meetings, reserves meeting rooms, and establishes meeting times and duration.

The team leader keeps meetings flowing and focused by doing the following:

- Keeping project objectives in front of the team
- Keeping process objectives in front of the team
- Identifying the product(s)
- Identifying the customer(s)
- Keeping meetings on schedule—not running over the allotted time without consensus
- Using the process chart for focus and structure

Team leaders also challenge the current process through these actions:

- Starting at the beginning of the chart
- Addressing each step, one at a time
  - Can we eliminate, combine, change sequence, change place, change person?
  - Is proposal practical?
  - Will it reduce costs, increase throughput, or improve quality?
- Posting ideas on the chart
- Striving for consensus by continually assessing ideas in terms of organization benefit
- Reviewing all recharted ideas
- Working with the team recorder to ensure that all ideas are captured and to assign information-gathering tasks to team members

Project Team Recorder

Project team recorders capture all the ideas generated at the meetings. A flipchart or board can help to ensure that all ideas are recorded. They also record task assignments. At the end of each meeting, they read through their meeting notes. Prior to the next meeting, they prepare a summary of the ideas generated in the last meeting and a list of assignments, which they review at the start of the meeting.

Installation Coordinator

The *installation coordinator* is often the same person as the project team leader. With the assistance of the project facilitator, the installation coordinator is responsible for seeing that the approved recommendations are properly installed, establishing a schedule of activities, monitoring them, and taking action as required to assure completion.

Process Performance Monitor

The *process performance monitor* is an employee with day-to-day involvement in the process. This person monitors performance of the process and identifies problems and opportunities for improvement. The process performance monitor becomes the process expert resource for other process performance monitors and project teams. They work with the Process Improvement Group to initiate improvement projects and validate current process charts on a routine basis. This person has general knowledge of the entire process and knows whom to contact for process details.

PROJECT OWNERSHIP: TRANSFERRING RESPONSIBILITY

The transfer of ownership in an improvement project is transparent. It happens smoothly, as long as the new owner(s), with guidance from the Process Improvement Group, recognize their responsibilities. An overview model of the transfer of ownership in a process improvement project is presented in Exhibit 2.1.

Projects may be conceived and conducted anywhere in an organization. Strategic business processes are defined and reviewed by the Executive Oversight Team. Process owners and process performance monitors keep tabs on business processes and subprocesses. Employees are routinely working with processes. Any one of these individuals or groups may identify a process for study. In organizations that have adopted process improvement into their culture, identifying opportunities for improvement may be expected from everyone. To begin with, the project idea is owned by its originator(s), but only until it is put into action.

The project idea is proposed by the originator to the process improvement champion, who works with a facilitator and the process owner to formalize a project agreement. The process improvement champion then owns the proposed project until it is handed off to an improvement project facilitator. The facilitator charts the process and familiarizes the project team members with the chart and with analysis techniques.

The project is then handed off to the project team leader, who is responsible for leading the project team members through process analysis. The facilitator is available for guidance but backs off the analysis. The project belongs to the team and the facilitator is there for support. The team develops improvements, prepares recommendations, performs benefit and cost analysis, develops a written proposal, and presents it to management.

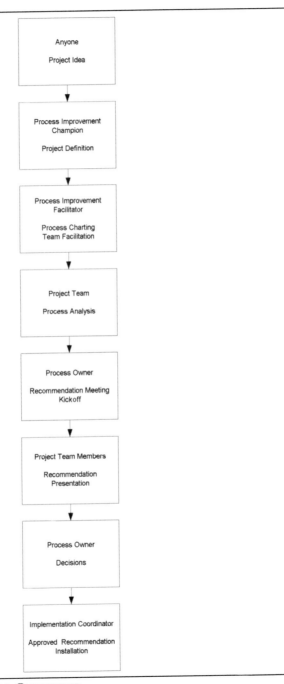

EXHIBIT 2.1 TRANSFERRING OWNERSHIP

The ownership of the project is then transferred to the process owner at the onset of the proposal presentation meeting. The process owner kicks off the meeting and then transfers ownership back to the team for a quick presentation of their recommendations. The team presents the recommendations and transfers ownership back to the process owner. The process owner and the other managers review, discuss, and ask questions about the recommendations. The meeting is concluded with a decision by the process owner on each recommendation, the assignment or approval of an installation coordinator, and appropriate commendations on the work completed.

With the close of the meeting, the ownership is passed to the installation coordinator, who will manage the implementation. The facilitator works with the installation coordinator to revise the process charts as the improvements are implemented and to see that the revised charts get to the process library manager and into the process chart library.

3

DEFINING A PROCESS IMPROVEMENT PROJECT

No wind blows in favor of a ship that has no port of destination.

—Michel de Montaigne

This is where you identify the process to be studied and establish the boundaries. Attending to a few administrative tasks up front will assure that the process owner is on board, that management's expectations are delineated, and that appropriate boundaries are set to guide the focus of the project team.

SELECT A PROCESS TO STUDY

A process study might be initiated by anyone in the organization. An employee who is involved in the process might challenge an existing method. A supervisor or manager might be concerned with an apparent problem in a process. Any number of red flags might point to a particular process for study. Customer complaints, a high error or defect rate, a too-lengthy process, high cost, high backlog, overtime—these are all issues that might trigger a process study.

However, fixing a problem is *not* a prerequisite for initiating a process study. A manager might just want to understand a process better, or might want to document a process to assist with training. A process might be targeted for review to meet regulatory or certification requirements. Any process that has not been reviewed for a while, when charted, will likely present opportunities for improvement that were not obvious before the chart was prepared.

When a process has been identified, the process owner (the lowest-level executive whose span of control covers the entire process) should decide whether to initiate a project. The process owner will ultimately approve any process changes, and the process owner will establish the objectives and scope of the project.

SECURE THE APPROVAL AND SUPPORT OF THE PROCESS OWNER

The process owner needs to be involved during two periods of a Process Improvement Project—at the onset of the project and at its conclusion. At the onset, the process owner will help develop the objectives and scope for the project and will make a formal announcement to the people who are involved in the process. The announcement will introduce the project facilitator, describe the objectives and scope of the project, ask for support, and offer support and encouragement. Introducing the project facilitator is helpful because the facilitator will soon be visiting the different work areas to interview people involved in the process, gathering the facts necessary to prepare a process chart.

With this announcement, the process owner can help to alleviate a principal concern that may be on the minds of everyone in the room with an honest statement that no one will be let go as a result of this process improvement effort. If the process owner cannot make this statement with conviction, it will likely be difficult to tap into the ingenuity and experience of the project team members to achieve positive results. In fact, their experience and expertise may be redirected to assuring that the project is *not* successful.

STATE THE PROCESS AND ITS PURPOSE

Simply stating a name for the process can help hone in on its purpose. We should ask ourselves, "What does this process do, and why are we doing it in the first place?" We identify the result or product of the process and challenge its value. Don't treat this step lightly; if there is not a good reason for doing the work, we should stop doing it. Lillian Gilbreth put this into excellent perspective with her comment, "There is too much study of work that should be eliminated, not studied."[1]

IDENTIFY THE TYPE OF PROJECT

Knowing the type of project will help you define it. Most improvement projects fit into one of six general categories:

1. Documentation project
2. Improvement project
3. Renewal project
4. Standardization project
5. Development project
6. Maintenance project

Documentation Project

In a documentation project, the current process is charted, validated, and approved. This may be to provide charts for training, to satisfy audit or certification requirements, or simply for building a library of process charts to serve as a foundation for a continuous improvement program. Try to carry these projects a step further. Improvement projects can help get people excited about project work and on board a continuous improvement program.

For example, when an executive in a major credit card company realized that the processes in its credit card department were not satisfactorily documented, managers decided to prepare detailed process charts of the major processes in the department. Subsequently, an internal audit resulted in an excellent report. Following that audit, the audit group customarily checked with the business improvement group to see if there were charts available for the area they were preparing to audit.

Improvement Project

Chart a process, review it with the people who do the work, and give them the opportunity to make any simple improvements. These kinds of quick improvements are sometimes alluded to as *picking the low-hanging fruit* or *picking up the pearls on the beach*. Examples include eliminating redundant copies of filed documents or stopping the distribution of reports to people who don't use them.

For example, a chemical company used detail process charts to document the processes it went through to secure patents on intellectual property. One small process involved a handoff of documentation from the U.S. Patent Group to the International Patent Group. Although the process was not particularly involved, it managed to create headaches for both groups. When a team of representatives reviewed the process together, both groups quickly understood the challenges the other group was facing. They worked out a good process very quickly, and both groups left with a new respect for the work the other group was doing.

Renewal Project

Chart a process, review it with a team of people who do the work, update the chart, and go through several iterations of review and update to develop an improved process. This is the common perception of an improvement project. Changes may be incremental or dramatic. They might include new technology, facilities, programming—or they might not. A renewal project might result in elimination of a lot of unnecessary work at very little cost or the purchase of expensive equipment and software. It might result in fewer people needed to do the work or the requirement to hire more people. The important thing is that the recommendations ultimately come from the team of people who do the work and who will have to live with the changes they make. (A team can confidently make recommendations to reduce staff knowing that employees will be reassigned and not released.)

A supplier of business forms developed a proprietary software system for managing forms inventories. As it brought this system online, problems surfaced and the company faced the loss of major accounts, including one large customer whose forms and other printing purchases amounted to more than $6 million a year. Its production, sales, and inventory processes were charted, and teams of its employees worked through the charts to develop modifications that would effectively integrate those processes with the new forms inventory management system. This was accomplished and the customer's business was retained. Subsequently, the charts were used again to support the integration of an enterprise resource planning (ERP) system.

Standardization Project

In a standardization project, multiple similar processes are documented and analyzed together to develop a single improved process or a set of more tightly aligned processes.

For example, a potash mining company in Canada purchased a phosphate mining company based in North Carolina. The shipping process was charted for both organizations. Team members from both organizations met to analyze the processes. Both charts were on the walls. They worked through one of the charts (while continually referring to the other), and in the course of a day had worked out a process that was better than either.

Development Project

A development project gives us an opportunity to chart and challenge the flow of a process that does not yet exist. It is an opportunity to actually engineer a business process at its inception. Working with a detailed chart forces people to think through the process comprehensively, catching much that would be overlooked without the chart.

For example, when a credit card company chose to get into the automobile insurance business, it developed the processes that would support its new venture using detailed process charts. The charts not only speeded up the project, but they enabled the project team to analyze and correct potential problems before they were implemented. The process charts they developed were hung on the walls of the new facility to help new employees understand the work.

Maintenance Project

The maintenance project is the backbone of continuous improvement. It is a scheduled review of an existing process chart with people who are involved in the process.

This review and update keeps the material in the process library fresh. When a process chart is completed, reviewed, and approved, it gets logged into the process chart library, and at the same time it is tagged with a review date. On the review date, the chart is printed and reviewed with the people who do the work—any minor changes are noted on the chart, which is then updated, validated, reapproved, and returned to the process library. Major changes or concerns that arise during a maintenance review may spawn an improvement or a renewal project.

ESTABLISH OBJECTIVES

Objectives establish for the team what the process owner expects from the project. If the reason the project was initiated was because of an apparent problem with the process, an objective would be to correct the problem. General objectives to streamline the work, reduce paperwork, and cut cycle time might also be specified. The team should review the objectives of the study and establish internal targets (not usually published outside the team) that exceed expectations. For processes that have never been reviewed with a detail process chart, this is usually far easier than it may seem.

For example, a food manufacturing company established a team to review a process within its R & D department. The vice president of R & D set as an objective a reduction in cycle time with a target of 15 percent. The team established a much more ambitious target for themselves that ultimately reduced cycle time by 85 percent.

Also, in the early days of cable TV, when a cable company process improvement team was given an objective to get its installation time down to the industry average from three weeks to one week (*Note*: What do you think of that for an objective? Let's see what improvements we can make to get ourselves to be average.) they eventually settled on a goal of one day. The team worked through several iterations of improvements that eventually got the installation time down to one day. What do you think it would have ended up with if its internal goal was one week?

DEFINE THE SCOPE

The project scope sets the boundaries and keeps the focus on the selected process. Set a start point and an end point, and identify the major items (e.g., documents, forms, systems) that support the process. Establishing the start and end point may not be as straightforward as it sounds. Take an order process, for example. To establish the start point, we ask, "What triggers this process? What causes us to start processing an order?" An obvious start point may be when the order department receives an order.

That sounds simple enough but might not be as clear when we actually observe the process. So we ask, "How is an order received?" or, more specifically, "How is the order information passed from the customer to the order department?" This may lead us to find that all orders are received on a standard order form via fax or mail—or that some customers simply send e-mail requests, or that multiple order forms are being used, or that orders may arrive electronically or by phone.

Even with orders arriving via several methods, we can still set the start point in the order department or back up in the process to the point where the organization receives the order (if it is not received in the order department)—or perhaps take it back even further to the customer at the point the order is originated. If the customer is an external person or organization, it might be difficult to include them in the study. However, you may discover opportunities for dramatic improvements by extending the process boundaries to include vendors and customers.

IDENTIFY THE PROJECT TEAM MEMBERS

The process tells us who should be on the improvement team. Team members will be knowledgeable employees who represent all of the work areas through which the process flows. One team member will be identified as the team leader, and another will be identified as the team recorder. (These roles may be determined by consensus of the team members at the first meeting.)

ENDNOTE

1.   Allan H. Mogensen, *Common Sense Applied to Motion and Time Study* (McGraw-Hill, 1932), 13.

4

GATHERING THE FACTS

Facts do not cease to exist because they are ignored.

—Aldous Huxley

Fact gathering is an integral part of understanding reality and preparing a good process chart. Yet, it is often dismissed or given cursory attention as superficial process charts are created by an individual or group of people some distance away from the work—and thereby some distance away from reality. If you want your process charts to reflect reality, you must go to the work and see it happen.

SET THE STAGE

There aren't many things you can do at the office that will make an employee more uncomfortable than having someone they don't know looking over their shoulder and taking notes. We should do everything we can to allay their concerns before we even get started. Data collection should be preceded with a public announcement by a respected, high-level executive. A single announcement by the executive whose span of control covers the process is ideal. This is the person we described as the process owner. This is the person who can ultimately make decisions about any part of the process. Enthusiastic support from this person will encourage cooperation from the people who do the work and discourage political posturing by managers who control portions of the process.

The purpose of this announcement is to inform the people who are involved in the process about the project and ask for their support. The executive will explain the objectives of the project and introduce the person who will collect the facts. The people will be asked to make time to support the project. They will be given an opportunity to ask questions, and they will be assured that there will be no loss of employment as a result of this process improvement effort.

COLLECT THE FACTS AT THE WORK AREA

It has become a fairly common practice to gather the people who do the work together in a room to build a process chart. While these are the right people to bring together to study and improve the process, this is not the best way to build an as-is chart. When people are away from their workplace, they tend to focus on the value-added steps they perform and often overlook many of the non–value-added steps that are apparent at the workplace. Also, it wastes the time of all the other people in the room while one person is explaining their work. We use less employee time and get better results if we wait until the as-is chart is complete and then bring a team of employees together to study and improve it.

Collect the facts at the work area. Period. Grab a clipboard and a pencil, and follow the process. There are a couple of ways that this can be accomplished, but all methods begin with clearing the work with the supervisors. Go through the appropriate channels on the first pass (visit the managers and supervisors and get the okay to deal directly with the people doing the work on future visits).

If the process is not too spread out, you can take a quick walk-through during which you get approval to deal directly with the people, get their names and phone numbers, and set up interviews.

An escort who is familiar with the process can make arrangements for people to be available and take care of introductions from one work location to the next. This can speed up the data collection noticeably.

When the process permits, it is easiest to follow the process from beginning to end observing an actual transaction. This isn't always feasible. Some processes take days, weeks, months, or even years to complete. When you can't observe an actual transaction, observe a simulated one (perhaps one that was recently completed or a hypothetical one)—but fill out the forms, access the system, get the signatures, make the photocopies, just like the real process.

Sometimes it is simply convenient to jump out of order. For instance, when one person handles a part of a process, and then passes the work on to another person who does something with it, then returns it to the first person. It might be easier to finish interviewing the first person before moving on to the next. Or an employee may be under pressure to complete something at the time you arrive to interview, so you simply find out when it will be convenient and come back later. If you were describing the work by simply writing paragraphs, this could easily lead to inadvertently leaving something out, but when you are drawing a detailed process chart, the chart itself provides good assurance that this won't happen.

INTERVIEW EXPERIENCED EMPLOYEES

If you want to find out how a job is done, ask someone who knows how to do it. Pretty simple advice, right? Yet it is amazing how often process charts, procedures, even custom software applications are developed some distance from reality—away from the people who actually do the work.

If you want to know how a job is done, look for the person or people who really know how to do it. You don't want someone who has to guess his or her way through the process. New hires, people who did the job years ago, people in adjacent departments—these are wrong people and this is not a criticism of their personal experience. They simply are not the best source of the experience that we are seeking. You want someone who knows it! Find the person that the other employees go to when they are stumped. This is the person who can show you the ropes. This is the person who can walk you through their part of the process and answer any questions you might have. This is the same person you will want to have on your analysis team.

Occasionally, a supervisor who is familiar with the work will want to explain the work to you. In some cases, the supervisor may be a good person to interview, the right person—if they have done the job for some time and are still involved in doing the work. However, if they have been away from it for a while, the scene might be something like this:

> The Interviewer says, "I'd like to talk with Emily, I understand she is the resident expert in this area." The supervisor replies, "Well, Emily is really swamped right now. I did that job for years. I can tell you what she does." Interviewer: "I'd really like to observe her doing the work." Supervisor: "She needs to finish the work she's doing by 2:00. I can show you what she does." Interviewer: "Okay." Supervisor: "She goes into the Patient Database, enters the patient name and assessment data..." Interviewer: "Excuse me, where does the patient information come from?" Supervisor: "Oh, that's in the Oasis package. She checks her entries..." Interviewer: "Excuse me again. What is the Oasis package?" Supervisor: "That's the mandated form that the nurse needs to complete when she goes out to visit a patient." Interviewer: "May I see one, please?"
>
> The supervisor may have to go to Emily's desk now to pick up an Oasis package. The interviewer will continue with the questions. The next questions may be, "Where does Emily get the Oasis package?...When is it dropped off?...Does she get more than one delivery per day?..When are the other deliveries?" Then the interviewer will want to see the patient database, specifically, the screens that are updated with the Oasis information. If the supervisor is not really comfortable with the current process, it probably won't be long before the interviewer is handed off to Emily.

The interviewer *was not* trying to be a pest with the supervisor. She was asking the same questions that she would ask Emily; only Emily would have the answers at hand.

You may hear that no two people do the job the same way. In fact, one person will probably do the same work differently at times. There is nothing wrong with charting a few alternative methods. Just stick with the experienced people. You don't have to identify every alternative method for doing the same work. If you capture the methods of the "best" workers, you will have a good baseline to work with.

BE GENUINE

Successful fact gathering requires a blend of social and technical skills. From a social standpoint, an interviewer doesn't want to appear threatening. Assume the role of fact finder—the people are the experts. Do what you can to help employees relax and be as comfortable as they can be with someone looking over their shoulder. Collect your notes with a pencil and paper (a recorder or computer device will be more threatening) and show the person your notes, explain what you are doing, reinforce what the executive said at the kickoff meeting, and show them the respect due someone who has something that you would like to learn. Make sure that employees understand what you are doing and why they are involved. They are the experts. It has to be sincere. The interviewer must have a true respect for the work knowledge of the employee or they will have difficulty getting the information they need.

A friendly, good-natured attitude along with an honest and open demeanor will help open the door for the interviewer. Then the interview must be conducted with professionalism. Respect work schedules and job-related interruptions. Let the employee know that if they need to answer the phone, they should answer the phone. You can wait. If something comes up that the person needs to attend to, you can come back. Work quickly. Capture the information that you need, clarify uncertainties, let the person know that you will be back later with a chart for them to validate, then move on.

When the interviewer arrives at an employee's workstation, the first thing the employee will likely do is turn toward the interviewer (away from the work). The interviewer should begin with an introduction and allow a few minutes of idle conversion. The interviewer will want to give the employee time to get comfortable with the situation. This might involve talk about the weather, a ball game, something in the news, whatever....Then the interviewer explains the data collection process. The interviewer may show the employee notes as they are being taken and offer to let the employee look them over when the interview is finished. The employee will probably start explaining what he or she does. It is the job of the interviewer at this point to turn the employee back toward the work and have the employee *demonstrate* what he or she does.

CAPTURE THE FACTS

The information that is introduced, used, and disseminated in our business processes doesn't float around in the air. It is either in people's heads or it is recorded on things—documents, forms, reports, e-mail, files, records, and so on. When information processes are charted, it is those things that are charted. The interviewer focuses on the things that drive the process. The interviewer moves through the process from one workstation to the next, collecting copies of completed forms, source documents, screen prints, and so on, that will help the team relate the process chart to the actual items that flow through the process and will provide detail of each entry of information that is recorded.

The charting symbols and conventions provide excellent shorthand for recording the data. Jot down a symbol and a few words to explain the activity and go on to the next step. If the task is repetitive, watch several iterations to validate your work and possibly capture variations and exceptions. Most importantly, get the facts from observation whenever possible. People can usually demonstrate the work faster than they can describe it, and demonstration is much closer to reality than words. (Try explaining how to tie a shoe without demonstration.) Be methodical: Follow and list the steps in order. Stick to identifying *what* happens at each step and avoid detail of *how* steps are performed. This saves an enormous amount of time.

When the person doing the work is adding information, identify the source of the information. If an entry is made and it is not apparent where the data came from, ask. If the answer is something like, "I have all the product codes memorized," then ask where a new person would find that information. This is another source. If the source for any piece of information that is required to complete a process exists only in the head of the person who does that part of the process, the organization is in a precarious position (with regard to completing this process). Prudent business behavior tells us to document the source or cross-train another employee to provide backup for this step. A step of this nature appears on the process chart as an entry of information without any apparent source or with words such as "provided by employee."

When the item being observed affects another item or spawns a new item, capture the other item. (On the process chart, the other item will be represented as another label and horizontal line.) This is an area where real talent can be developed. The interactions between different documents are what tie items together to become a single process.

Identify the person (*who*) you are interviewing and the work area location (*where*). These won't change until you move on to the next work area. Identify the start point and end point for this piece of the process (e.g., the process starts with an in-basket full of orders after the first mail delivery around 8:30 each morning, each order is entered into the system and then set aside for filing). Start with the activity that triggers the work (orders placed in the in-basket) and then watch the employee process the work.

Ask employees to *show* you what they do: Fill out the form, review the order, update the database, send the e-mail, make the copy, print the report—whatever they do. Note *what* is done at each step and get an estimate of the *amount of time* associated with each delay and any time-consuming steps.

Avoid getting into detail of HOW each step is performed. Answers to the other questions provide us with enough detail to provide proper focus on the step for analysis of the process. For most activities, *how* is answered briefly (e.g., written with a pen, keyed) by the activity (symbol) and the item (label). In many cases, *how* could fill pages and still not be adequate. It can involve a great deal of skill developed through training and experience at doing the task that is a single step on the chart. Rather than trying to record all of this detail, involve the person with the detailed knowledge of how the work is performed in the analysis.

The past several pages have dealt with *how* to collect data to build a process chart. These paragraphs have outlined details of skills used when interviewing people to obtain the data necessary to prepare a good process chart. If you were charting the data collection process itself, all of this would be represented with a single Add-Alter or Origination symbol with a description like "process data written."

Finally, never ask *why*. Why is evaluative and causes people to become defensive. It isn't necessary to know why at this point. Save why for analysis when it becomes the most important question.

LEVEL OF DETAIL

A few guidelines can help you get a feel for how much detail to capture. When the symbol changes, capture it. When the source changes, capture it. The Handling symbol occurs most often on most charts. There are usually handling operations before and after transports, before and after delays, and before and after sets of value-added symbols and inspections. Digging into the level of detail addresses the question *how*? If you focus on *what* is happening and not on the details of *how* it is done, the data collection will be easier and quicker, and your chart will be easier to work with.

As an example, a filing step is typically (and appropriately) denoted with a single Handling symbol. However, there can be a lot more detail in that simple step. The person scoots his or her chair back, bends over, and pulls the file drawer out. The person rifles through the file tabs to the appropriate file folder and pulls that folder. Then the employee jogs the folder behind the one pulled to mark the place. He or she inserts the document into the pulled folder and files it back in the drawer, repositioning the jogged folder. The drawer is closed and the person readjusts the chair.

All of these details are part of filing. There are no steps in this scenario that are anything but handling. We aren't studying motions, we are studying process. Adding more detail will clutter the chart rather than clarify it. The person doing the work will be a part of the analysis team that studies this process step and will have more detail than we can put in the chart.

What about the work a person does when accessing different screens in a computer? This depends on the focus of a project. If a program is a primary focus of the project (there exists an opportunity to make changes to the program), you can chart interface with the program in detail, capturing each screen or window as a separate item line. On the other hand, if the program is not a focus of the project or there will be no opportunity to make changes to the application, then it can be charted as a single item line.

If, later during analysis, a step is discovered that warrants more detail charting, you can and should go back and chart it in more detail.

ORGANIZE THE FACTS WITH A PROCESS FLOW CHART

Once the data have been collected, build a process chart. Don't let the notes sit. If you sleep on them, you will lose some of the information. The longer you delay, the more you will lose.

Every item that is observed in the process will be represented as a horizontal line that begins with a label to identify the item. The work steps that happen to each item are identified with symbols that are placed along the line in the sequence that they occur. Charts flow left to right to imply the sequence of the steps over time. Relationships between items are shown with V-shape effects that point from the line of the source item into a symbol that shows what is happening to the affected document represented by another line.

After you have captured your notes in a process chart, you (and anyone else involved in the process) will be able to come back to the chart days, weeks, or months later and understand detailed workings of the process!

5

PROCESS CHART FORMAT

*The process chart is a device for visualizing a process as a means of improving it.
Every detail of a process is more or less affected by every other detail; therefore the
entire process must be presented in such form that it can be visualized all at once
before any changes are made in any of its subdivisions.*
—Frank B. Gilbreth and Lillian M. Gilbreth

Process charts display all of the major items in a process. They show what happens
to each item, step by step, and where items affect each other.

PROCESS CHARTS FLOW LEFT TO RIGHT

Process implies movement, and movement is depicted as a line drawn left to right.
The movement through a process is the *process flow* and can be followed by reading the chart from left to right.

Charts are tools that are meant to be read. A moderately complex chart, drawn
at a scale large enough for a group of people to work on it together, may be 10 feet
long, 20 feet long, or even longer. If it were vertical, it would necessarily sprawl
out over the floor. As a horizontal chart, it can be put on a wall at eye level, and a
team can read through it and work with it.

Process flow charts flow left to right and tend to be long and narrow. The horizontal nature of a detail process chart is shown in Exhibit 5.1. If this chart were
printed as a wall chart, it would be six to eight feet long. Obviously, as presented
here, this chart is not legible; however, even at this scale, with just a little instruction a number of facts can still be derived from this chart. There are 15 different
items involved in this process, including one item that is separated into four items.
One of the four items will follow one of four alternative paths and then join up
with another of the four items. One of the four items is simply filed and held while
the last is joined with the trigger item that kicked off the process. We can also see
that four items are created during the process and that not one of the items in the
process is discarded or deleted. Granted, this is not particularly useful information

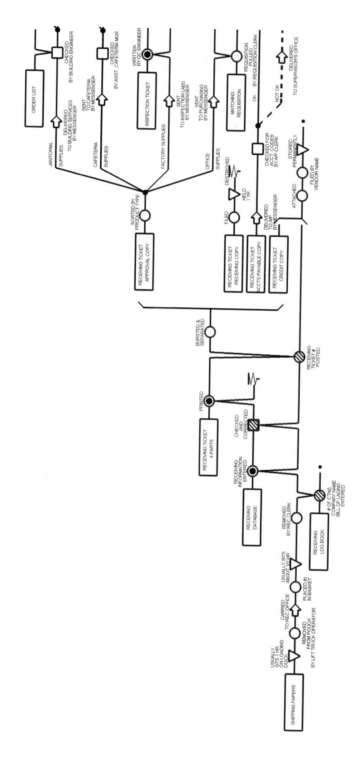

EXHIBIT 5.1 HORIZONTAL FLOW OF A DETAIL PROCESS CHART

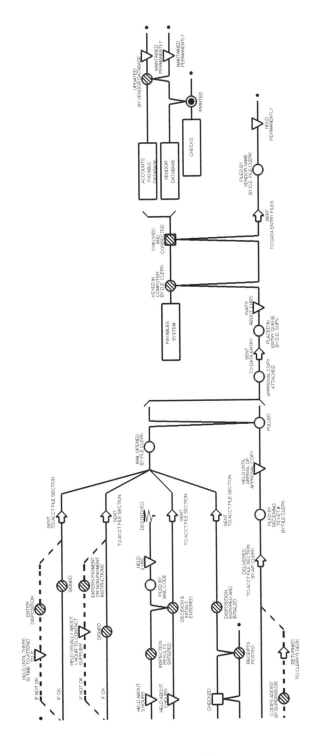

EXHIBIT 5.1 HORIZONTAL FLOW OF A DETAIL PROCESS CHART *(CONTINUED)*

33

as presented, but in front of an improvement team who would have the benefit of being able to read the item names as well as the actions, this level of detail is particularly valuable.

Most charting methodologies do not come close to providing this level of detail in a single picture. The point of process flowcharting is to provide a visual representation of the process including each item in the process.

EVERY ITEM IS CHARTED AS A SEPARATE FLOW LINE

Detail process charts depict the recording of information and the flow of recorded information; the handling, updating, reviewing, and moving of the media on which the information is recorded. These media are referred to as items and are represented by item lines. They are the physical entities that are charted as they flow through the process. An item is identified with a label at the beginning of a horizontal line that represents the process flow of that item. An item is always something physical. It is something you can see. This includes electronic files, e-mail, documents, diskettes, CDs, databases, log books, reference books, and so on. Process charts can also include item lines that are not documents such as products, parts of products, people, and so on. Detail process charts are also referred to as *multiflow charts*.

PROCESS CHARTS SHOW THE INTERRELATED FLOWS OF MANY ITEMS

It is difficult to make changes to one item in a business process without affecting other items. Process charts clearly show the relationships between items with a V-shaped convention called an *effect*. Relationships between items tie the pieces of the process (all the different items) together. These relationships show when information on one item is used to cause something to happen to another item.

Brackets show when items are combined or separated. When a four-part form is separated into four individual items, an opening bracket is used to show a single flow line splitting into four separate flow lines. Each of the four new flow lines begins with a label for identification. When a form is placed into a project folder or several documents are attached, a closing bracket is used. The flow lines terminate at the closing bracket and a single flow line continues out of the bracket.

EVERY ITEM IS LABELED

A *label* at the beginning of each flow line tells us what is flowing through that flow line. All of the steps along a single flow line are happening to that item. Exhibit 5.2 shows a section of a chart that includes a number of different items involved in a patenting process. New process lines are introduced when the *patent database* is accessed, when the *International Instruction Sheet* is printed from the patent database, and when the *activities screen* is displayed. A new line is also introduced for

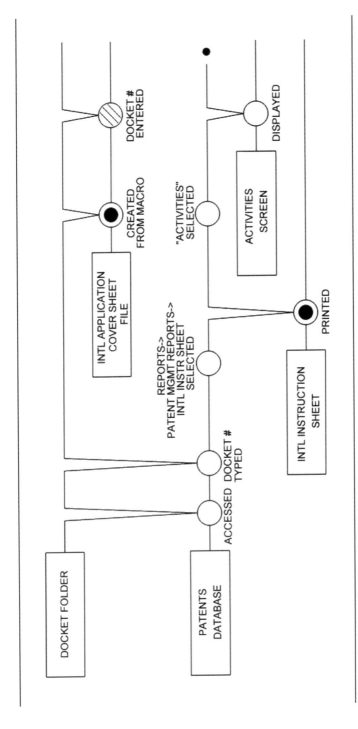

EXHIBIT 5.2 A LABEL FOR EVERY ITEM

35

the *International Application Cover Sheet* that is created. Every line begins with a label. Every action that occurs on an item line is happening to the item identified in the label.

The labels serve as a *table of contents* for the chart. Read the labels and you will know all the major items involved in the process.

ACTIONS AND NONACTION STEPS ARE INDICATED BY SYMBOLS LAID OUT IN SEQUENCE ALONG EACH FLOW LINE

Symbols that indicate the steps, actions, or operations that happen to the named item appear sequentially along the process flow line. Each symbol includes a few words to complete the description of what is happening to the item at that step. Periods of nonactivity are captured using the *delay symbol.*

CORRECTION AND REJECTION ROUTINES ARE SHOWN WITH DOTTED LINES

Sometimes the items being processed are inspected. Processing that occurs when an item fails an inspection (a control point) is indicated on the chart as a dotted line.

FUNDAMENTAL NATURE OF THE PROCESS CHART FORMAT

Process charts display what people do, step by step, to the items in a process. The flow lines represent the items, and the symbols represent the actions. Each item is distinct and each step is distinct, so there is little confusion about just what is happening and what it is happening to at every point in the process.

6

PROCESS CHART BUILDING BLOCKS

*The process chart is admirably suited to the study of paperwork systems
and procedures. For such analyses, the usual chart is made to portray the flow
of each copy of a multicopy form. Then, the chart for each copy is redrawn on paper
of sufficient size, leaving spaces for noting actions taken on other papers and
records affected.*

—American National Standard ANSI Y15.3M-1979

The building blocks of a process chart are symbols, conventions, and words. The
symbols represent actions. The conventions represent the items and show the process
flow and how the actions are tied together. The words help clarify answers to
the questions of what, who, where, and when for each step.

SYMBOLS: THE ACTIONS

The work simplification symbols represent the action and nonaction steps (the
verbs) in a process. The identification of nonaction steps, which account for most
of the processing time (typically more than 95 percent), distinguishes the work
simplification approach from most others. Each step in a work process is identified
by one of eight symbols.

The real beauty of the symbol set lies in its design, simple yet comprehensive.
The four base symbols shown in Exhibit 6.1 provide a powerful common language
for describing work.

○	⇨	☐	▽
OPERATION	TRANSPORTATION	INSPECTION	STORAGE/DELAY

EXHIBIT 6.1   FOUR BASE SYMBOLS

37

Operations show when work is being done. Transportations show when the work moves from one workplace to another. Inspections show when work is checked. The storage/delay symbol shows when nothing is happening.

This outstanding set of categories is analogous to an alphabet or number system in that it meets the requirements for being a powerful, working set. The symbols are mutually exclusive, comprehensive, and universally applicable:

- *Mutually exclusive.* Each symbol represents a distinct type of action. Therefore, the categories do not overlap, which would make it difficult to determine which symbol to apply. An item is either moving (an arrow) or stationary (all other symbols); it is either doing nothing (a triangle) or doing something (all other symbols), and so on.
- *Comprehensive.* They cover the work processes completely. There are no spaces between the categories of activities that are left uncovered.
- *Universally applicable.* They apply in all work areas. Therefore, it is not necessary to use different terminology in different work areas (i.e., legal, accounting, sales, engineering, IT, etc.).

This set of four symbols is rounded out with the inclusion of four more—all of which are variations of the circle symbol, doing work.

Three of these symbols (shown in Exhibit 6.2) represent physical change to an item. These are the *value-added steps.* Value-added steps change an item, making it closer to a finished product.

The Do operation covers all of the value-added steps in physical work processes—cutting, polishing, drilling, and so on. The Origination and Add/Alter symbols cover all of the value-added steps in information processing. In information processing, value-added steps are those steps where information is added or changed, bringing the item closer to completion.

The term *value added*, when used in the context of a process, has meaning that is limited to progress in the process. A physical change is made to a product or information on a document, in either case moving that item in the direction of being completed. The steps may not actually add any value to the item in the sense of being a better product or document. These steps that qualify as value added by the process definition may prove to be completely unnecessary or, in fact, the item itself may prove to be useless—but this is a decision to be made during analysis by the experts, the people who do the work. The Operation symbol represented by the

DO OPERATION   ORIGINATION   ADD/ALTER

EXHIBIT 6.2   VALUE-ADDED SYMBOLS

DESTROY

EXHIBIT 6.3 DESTROY SYMBOL

open circle, sometimes referred to as a *handling operation,* shows activities of doing work that do not add value.

The final symbol, the Destroy symbol (see Exhibit 6.3) represents the termination of an item in a process. For example, a product is trashed or a document is shredded.

Do

The Do symbol represents a physical change to a product, moving it in the direction of being completed. It shows value added in a *production* process (a physical change to an item that makes it closer to a finished product). The Do symbol is not used in information flows, but it may be used on charts that display both information flow and the processing of products.

Action words associated with a Do operation symbol tell the reader what is happening to a physical product. Some examples of words that would be associated with a Do symbol are

- Drilled
- Milled
- Turned
- Painted
- Polished
- Sanded

Exhibit 6.4 shows a short segment of a ceramic manufacturing process. The segment picks up this process after talc, clay, and water have been mixed and are waiting to be pressed into tile. Several setup steps occur: the powder is scooped into the shaker and shaken into the die, and the dies are engaged. Then the first value-added step occurs as the tile is pressed into shape. The tile is ejected from the die and moved forward to the next station, where the second value-added step occurs—the edges of the tile are sanded.

Although Do steps are critical to the throughput of manufacturing processes, they typically account for a very small percentage (2 percent or so) of the processing time.

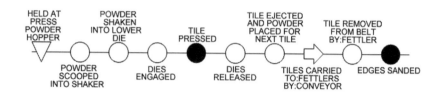

EXHIBIT 6.4 DO SYMBOL: VALUE-ADDED IN A MANUFACTURING PROCESS

Originate

The Origination symbol represents the first time information is entered on a document. This symbol shows added value in an information process (addition of information to an item that enables it to move on in the current process).

Action words associated with an Origination symbol tell the reader what is happening to a document. Some examples of words that would be associated with an Origination symbol are

- Filled in
- Completed
- Written
- Prepared
- Printed
- Copy made

This text might include a list of specific entries:

- Name and address entered
- Product code, description, and quantity written

Origination symbols show us at a glance where items are introduced into the process and can point to opportunities for significant productivity improvement and proportional error reduction. Often, when an improvement team looks at all of the documents that are originated in a process, they are able to come up with changes that eliminate many of them completely. Of course, when an origination step is eliminated, all of the other steps that follow for that document are also eliminated.

A new item is introduced to the process whenever a copy is made, even though all of the information on the copy is the same as the information of the document that was copied. The copy exists as a new document that will have its own flow. This means a new item line is needed with the first step an Origination symbol as shown by the customer order copy in Exhibit 6.5.

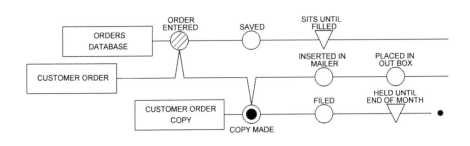

EXHIBIT 6.5   ORIGINATE SYMBOL: MAKING A COPY

When we print a hard copy of an e-mail, we have an electronic copy and a paper copy—two flow lines with the paper copy created (printed) from the electronic copy, as shown in Exhibit 6.6.

When we create an e-mail and send it to someone, a copy of the original e-mail is transmitted to the recipient and the original is likely stored in a Sent Mail folder, as shown in Exhibit 6.7.

Since an Origination symbol represents *the first time* information is entered on a document, there can be no more than one Origination symbol on a process line. Also, a process line will not always have an Origination symbol. Some items originate *before* they enter the process being charted. For example, if we chart an order process beginning with the receipt of the order, the order form will have been originated by the customer prior to the point where our chart begins unless we actually include the work done in the customer's office.

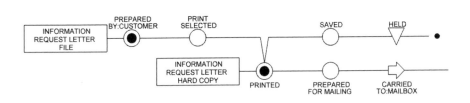

EXHIBIT 6.6   ORIGINATE SYMBOL: PRINTING A HARD COPY

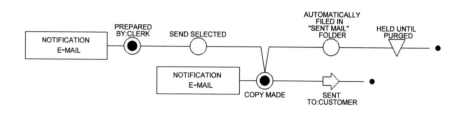

EXHIBIT 6.7 ORIGINATE SYMBOL: SENDING AN E-MAIL

There are situations where information is added to an existing item (e.g., log, table, database). In these situations, the items are not being originated; they are being appended with additional information. We will also display the source items that provide information. These items usually already exist before they appear in the process. Exhibit 6.8 shows four items (three source documents and one document being updated). The ownership reports, title opinions, and oil law records are all existing documents that are not modified during the process. The e-mail was originated by the sender, which may be reflected at a point earlier in the process.

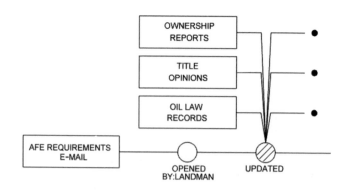

EXHIBIT 6.8 NOT ALL LINES ARE ORIGINATED IN THE PROCESS

Add/Alter

The Add/Alter symbol represents any time information is *added to* or *altered* on an item after the first entries. This symbol and the Origination symbol cover all of the times information is changed and, thus, they cover all of the value-added steps associated with items in an information process.

Action words associated with an Add/Alter symbol tell the reader what is happening to a document. Some examples of words that would be associated with an Add/Alter symbol are

- Signed
- Updated
- Corrected
- Dated
- Edited
- Entered

Add/Alter symbols show any change of information. It may be a date stamp, initials, signature, or even deletion or erasure of a previous entry.

Exhibit 6.9 shows the inspection of a document (a request for overtime pay) by a district commander with three possible outcomes. Following the top line, the problem is explained on the document and the document is returned to the sergeant. The middle line shows that the district commander corrects the problem, then the process rejoins the OK line to be signed off. If the document is OK, it is simply signed off.

The text associated with an Add/Alter symbol may include a list of specific entries. Exhibit 6.10 shows a list of entries into a log book.

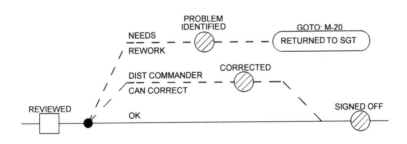

EXHIBIT 6.9 ADD/ALTER SYMBOL

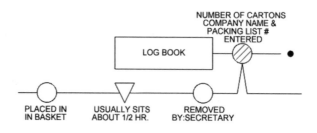

EXHIBIT 6.10   ADD/ALTER SYMBOL: LISTING SPECIFIED ENTRIES

Handle

The Handling symbol represents the activities in an information process that do not involve information change. They include physical paper shuffling and electronic paper shuffling (i.e., keying through electronic documents, application screens, and so on). There are usually more of these symbols on charts than any other. In production work, these symbols represent make-ready and put-away tasks associated with a job.

Action words associated with a Handling symbol tell the reader what is happening. Some examples of words that would be associated with a Handling symbol are

- Loaded
- Assembled
- Sorted
- Removed
- Unloaded
- Disassembled
- Attached
- Separated

Handling operations are typically the most common symbol on a chart, and since they are not adding value to items being processed, they are attractive opportunities for streamlining. Handling steps are also the steps that are most often overlooked during fact gathering. It is easy to mentally combine handling steps with other steps. The action of filing is easily visualized as a part of the storage symbol—for example. The actions of picking up a document, transporting it, then putting it back down might all be seen a part of the transportation step. Likewise, picking up a document to edit it can be seen as part of the value-added step. A conscious effort should be made to capture these steps that provide us with clues to improvement opportunity. Handling steps usually occur before and after transportation, before and after delays, before and after groups of value-added steps, and prior to the final storage symbol that occurs at the end of many process lines. The process segment in Exhibit 6.11 includes a number of handling steps. The bottom line includes a physical filing step prior to a two-year storage. All the other handling steps in this process segment are electronic. They include opening the customer account system and keying to the account maintenance screen where information is added, then saving and exiting the program. (When a keystroke is used for access but does not add information to a document, it calls for a Handling symbol and not an Add/Alter symbol.)

The level of detail that is captured in an electronic process can vary, depending on the type of project the chart is supporting and the opportunity the improvement team has to make modifications to the system. For instance, if the chart is being created to use as a training tool or if the system can be modified, then a detailed presentation is appropriate. If the chart is being prepared to support the integration of current processes with a new system, then a less detailed chart that focuses on the value-added steps might be considered (see Exhibit 6.12). Notice that the step to set up the new account is represented with an Add/Alter symbol in this case. In this process segment, the flow line represents the entire system that is being added to. In the previous chart segment, the separate flow line represented the individual record. Keep in mind that there is little more time-investment required to prepare the more detailed chart.

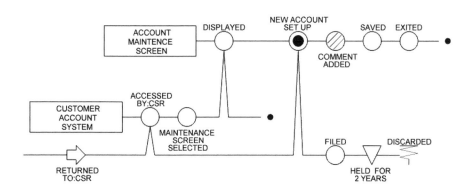

EXHIBIT 6.11   HANDLING SYMBOL

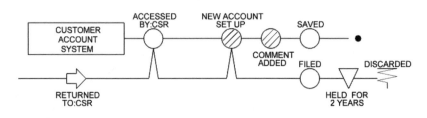

EXHIBIT 6.12   HANDLING SYMBOL: A HIGHER-LEVEL CHART OF AN ELECTRONIC PROCESS

In manufacturing processes, the steps to set up and clean up the equipment and the activities of collecting, grouping, and organizing parts together at the work area are all Handling operations.

Transportation

The Transportation symbol represents movement from one work area to another. It is *not* used for small movements that occur within a work area. Its purpose is to show movements between work areas that are physically separated, such that the employees are not in direct contact with each other as they work. These movements are often time-consuming and costly.

Transportation symbols are accompanied by words of movement, along with the destination. Some examples of words that would be associated with a Transportation symbol are

- Carried to accounting
- Sent to vendor
- Mailed to home office
- Walked to purchasing

When this symbol is used consistently, a person reading a chart can easily determine the answer to the question *where* at every step in the process. If the person preparing the chart indicates the location at the first symbol on the chart, the arrows will take care of all changes of location thereafter. All that is required is to check back to the last transportation and read the destination, or if there are no transportations, read the location at the first symbol.

The process segment shown in Exhibit 6.13 is from an actual process: Do you see anything silly in those steps?

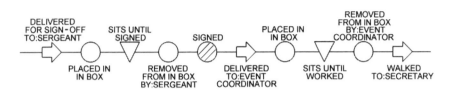

EXHIBIT 6.13   TRANSPORTATION SYMBOL

The events coordinator doesn't do anything with this item (a timesheet) except pass it on to the secretary. Did the sergeant have to walk past the secretary to get to the event coordinator's desk? Certainly a team of experienced employees would know. If so, the team would recommend delivering directly to the secretary, which would shorten that delivery and eliminate four other steps.

One situation that is mistakenly represented as transportation is when an item is passed from one person to another within the same workspace. There is an inherent confusion in this situation that associates the person change with a transportation. A Transportation symbol represents a change of location beyond the immediate work area. For instance, a customer and a counter clerk may exchange forms at the counter several times during a process. Because they are working together at the same workspace, the exchanges are all handling operations. If the counter clerk leaves the counter to obtain an approval or pick up a printout or for any reason, the materials that travel with the clerk are being transported.

Inspection

The Inspection symbol represents checking work to see if it is right or okay to continue. It is not used when checking is limited to normal, conscientious work. The purpose of this symbol is to show tasks that are specifically checking the work for correctness. Inspection symbols are typically followed by Correction routines that show alternative processing if the item fails the inspection. (The right angles of the square remind us that the symbol represents checking to see if the item is right.)

Action words associated with an Inspection symbol describe checking the work. Some examples of words that would be associated with an Inspection symbol are

- Checked
- Verified
- Proofed
- Reviewed
- Compared to standard
- Inspected

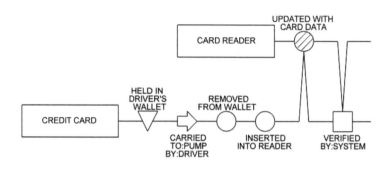

EXHIBIT 6.14   INSPECTION SYMBOL

The words associated with an Inspection symbol may include reference to a quality standard, specification, and so on.

One area that causes confusion in applying an Inspection symbol involves terminology. It occurs when one item is being "checked" to validate another. Take the case of validating a credit card (see Exhibit 6.14). The card is inserted into a reader and the system looks up the card to see if it is valid. This may commonly be expressed in language like, "We are checking the system to see if the card is valid." This can cause confusion. Where does the Inspection symbol go? Does it go on the system line or on the card line? Remember, you are checking to see if the item is okay. In this scenario, are you checking to see if the system is okay or if the card is okay? If the inspection is not passed, which item failed? Did the system fail, or did the card fail? Was the system bad or was the card bad? The symbol belongs on the line of the card. If the card is invalid, we stop the transaction. The card may be held or destroyed or returned—but it will not be processed. The system has been used only as a lookup tool.

Storage/Delay

The Storage/Delay symbol represents time when nothing happens to the item being charted. How small a period of time we choose to display on our charts is a matter of judgment. We should show storages and delays that consume significant amounts of time, and this will vary for different processes. (Sometimes a "D" symbol is used to distinguish a delay from storage. The location of the symbol and the description that accompanies it define the time expenditure with much more precision than simply storage or delay. In either case, the symbol simply means that nothing is happening.) Generally speaking, if the symbol occurs within a process line, it is a delay, and processing will continue following the delay. If it occurs at the end of a process line, it is storage. Sometimes storage may be followed by further longer-term, retention-related processing (moving off-site, filming, destruction, etc.).

Words associated with a Storage/Delay symbol describe nonactivity. They tell us the duration of the nonactivity or the condition that will end the nonactivity. Examples of words that tell us *how long* the period of nonactivity usually lasts include

- Held indefinitely
- Retained for one year

Examples of words describing conditions that end a Delay are

- Sits overnight
- Held until 3:00 p.m.

Most processing time is consumed waiting. In fact, currently, most documents in your organization are doing just that—nothing. Most of those are stored items and are doing exactly what they should be doing. However, there are also documents that somebody could use right now that are sitting someplace doing nothing. Process charts make these delays obvious, resulting in ideas for reducing processing time.

In Exhibit 6.15, the first delay shows an item sitting in an in basket. The process clearly isn't finished. The time frame is unclear but does indicate work in progress (it may be minutes or days, and we may want to narrow that down during analysis). The second occurrence is storage. It shows a retention period of two years, followed by destruction.

Often, Storage is the last symbol in the process. This is a sensible endpoint for a process although it may ignore retention-related processing. The Storage symbol should indicate duration, which will tell us if there is a retention policy in place (as in the example) or if the filing *is* the final resting place until some arbitrary purge, where the description might read "HELD INDEFINITELY."

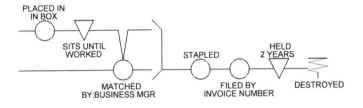

EXHIBIT 6.15   DELAY SYMBOL: DELAY AND STORAGE

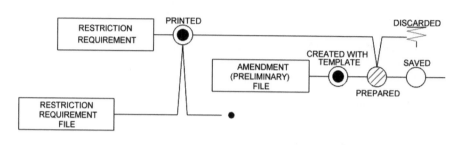

EXHIBIT 6.16   DESTROY SYMBOL

Destroy

The Destroy symbol represents an activity that causes the item to cease to exist. Its purpose is to show activities of purging and cleansing that are built into a system.

The words that accompany the Destroy symbol tell what is happening to the work. Some examples of words that would be associated with a Destroy symbol are

- Shredded
- Discarded
- Trashed
- Thrown away

When they are used, the Destroy symbols appear as the last step at the end of a flow line. Destruction of items is a function that is typically given less attention than it deserves. As a result, bureaucracies wind up with massive accumulations of nonessential and duplicate records. Electronics has not necessarily helped us here. It is too easy to save electronic files (i.e., e-mails, copies of letters and other documents, downloaded materials) and forget about them. However, vital records are sometimes destroyed. A well-prepared process chart shows clearly where each record goes and makes it easy to arrive at reasonable retention decisions.

In Exhibit 6.16, a document is printed, used as a source document to prepare an electronic document, then discarded.

COMBINATION SYMBOLS

Some situations involve a back-and-forth shifting between different types of activity. For instance, when a document is being edited, the activity might shift many times between Inspection and Correction. The checking activity and the correcting activity are difficult to separate. Certainly the checking activity comes before the correcting activity. However, the number of iterations can vary from document to

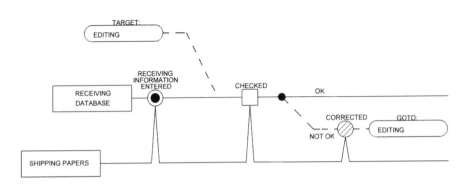

EXHIBIT 6.17   LOOPING PROCESS

document. Exhibit 6.17 shows how this could be displayed with a loop in the process. The entries are checked, and if they are not OK, we follow the dotted line path
to correct the entries, then loop back by following the Go-to connector to the Target connector, where we reenter the process to continue checking until the document is OK.

A simpler way to show this is with a combination symbol, as shown in Exhibit 6.18.

CONVENTIONS: CONNECTING THE SYMBOLS

We use the word *convention* to refer to the *conventional ways that we label and
draw the lines* that connect the symbols. There are also conventions that don't
relate directly to the process flow, but simply provide clarity to the chart. An item
is represented with a horizontal line. Symbols are placed along the line to represent
the activities of that item in the sequence in which they occur. Item lines begin
with a label for identification.

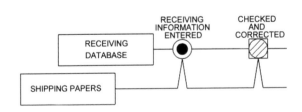

EXHIBIT 6.18   COMBINATION SYMBOL

A basic process flow is represented with a horizontal line, beginning with a label:

- *Line.* A line drawn left to right is used to display flow. The reader follows the movement of items through a process by reading the chart from left to right.
- *Label.* A label is a rectangular box that is placed at the beginning of each flow line. The document name is written inside the label and identifies the item that flows through the steps along that process line.

Documenting a process almost always requires charting the flow of *more than one item*. The following conventions show interrelationships between multiple flow lines:

- *Effect.* An effect shows a relationship between two items. One item provides information that causes something to happen to the other item.
- *Brackets.* Brackets show the physical gathering or separating of multiple items. Opening brackets show the separation of items. Closing brackets show the gathering of items.

The following conventions are used in individual flow lines:

- *Alternative.* Sometimes an item reaches a point in the process where information on the item will determine which path to follow. That point in the process is called a *Decision Point*. This convention is displayed as a small, solid circle with two or more alternative paths continuing out of it to the right.
- *Correction/Rejection.* A Correction or Rejection convention is a special case of alternative that follows an inspection. It displays the steps of a failed inspection and is shown as a dotted line extending to the right from a Decision Point.
- *Rejoin.* A Rejoin convention simply brings alternative paths back into a single line.

The following conventions are features that add clarity to a chart:

- *Connector label.* A Connector label at the end of a line is called a Go-to connector and indicates that processing continues either on another chart or somewhere on the same chart. The Go-to connector references a Target connector. The Target connector uses a Rejoin into another line to show where the processing continues.
- *Stop/Start.* A Stop/Start convention is used to indicate a section of processing that has been intentionally left out of a chart.
- *Period.* A Period is used on process lines the same way that it is used in a sentence; it marks the end of the line.
- *Bypass.* A Bypass is used to eliminate confusion at crossed lines.

Label and Line

A flowchart is a snapshot of a moving picture. Flow is displayed along a horizontal line. The line begins with a *label* that identifies the item that is represented by that line. Items are the physical entities that are charted as they flow through the process. An item is always something physical: It can be, for example, a document or group of documents, a file, an e-mail, a CD, a database, a product, a part of a product, a piece of material, or a person. Symbols are placed along the line representing the activities that happen to *that item*. The reader follows the flow by reading along the line from left to right.

Everything that happens along the flow line in Exhibit 6.19 happens to the shipping papers. In process language, the label is a noun and tells us the subject, and the symbols are the verbs that tell us the activity. The illustration reads like this:

1. The shipping papers sit on the loading dock about one hour.
2. The shipping papers are removed from the pouch by the lift truck operator.
3. The shipping papers are carried to the office.
4. The shipping papers are placed in the in basket.
5. The shipping papers usually sit in the in basket about one half hour.

Since we know that all the steps are associated with the shipping papers, we can prepare a more streamlined narrative:

The shipping papers sit on the loading dock about one hour. They are removed from the pouch by the lift truck operator, who carries them into the office and places them in the in basket where they will sit for about one half hour.

A simplistic flow of a single item can be drawn with a label and a few symbols along a horizontal line. However, most information flows involve multiple items. When there are multiple items involved in a process, every item is represented with its own line—and each line begins with a label (see Exhibit 6.20). The labels provide a knowledgeable reader with a table of contents for the chart—they identify all the documents in the process.

Notice that all the lines are tied or grouped together. Effects and brackets show the relationships between multiple items.

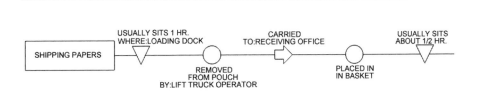

EXHIBIT 6.19 LANGUAGE STRUCTURE OF PROCESS CHARTS

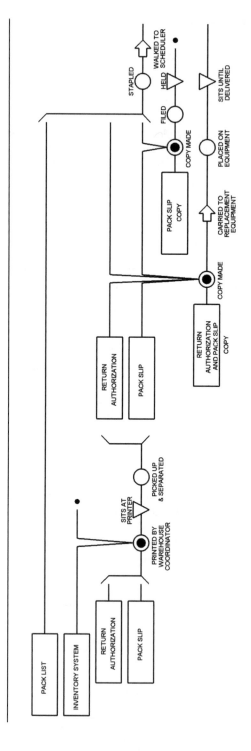

EXHIBIT 6.20 LABELS PROVIDE A TABLE OF CONTENTS FOR THE CHART

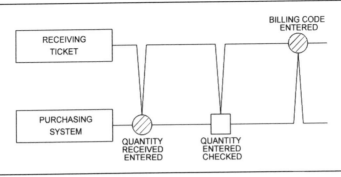

EXHIBIT 6.21   EFFECT CONVENTION

Effect

An *effect* is drawn as a V that points up or down from one item line into a symbol on another item line. The effect shows that information from one item is being used to cause something to happen—an action (shown with a symbol) on another item line. The open end of the effect is always at the line supplying the information. The point of the effect is always at a symbol that shows what is being done to the affected item.

In Exhibit 6.21, the receiving ticket supplies the quantity information that is entered into the purchasing system. Then the quantity on the receiving ticket is used once more to validate the entry that was just made into the purchasing system (the entry into the purchasing system is checked). Then a billing code that is provided by the purchasing system is written on the receiving ticket.

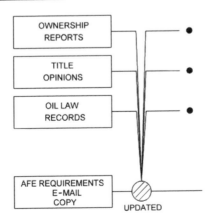

EXHIBIT 6.22   MULTIPLE EFFECTS INTO A SINGLE SYMBOL

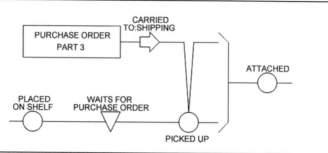

Exhibit 6.23 Combining Items

Multiple items can supply information that affects a single item. Exhibit 6.22 shows three documents providing information to update an authorization for expenditure (AFE) requirements e-mail.

An effect shows an interaction between two items. In the previous example, there is an effect between each of the source documents and the AFE requirements e-mail.

Brackets

Brackets are used to show grouping and ungrouping of multiple items. Groupings may be physical or logical.

Physical Grouping. The closing bracket shows multiple item lines being grouped together to continue the flow along a single line. In Exhibit 6.23, the closing bracket shows items being *physically* assembled. The closing bracket shows separate paths being combined into a single path. The Handle symbol directly following the closing bracket represents the activity of assembling the documents.

An opening bracket is used when documents that are moving through the process flow together are physically separated into multiple flow lines. The opening bracket is immediately followed by labels that identify the items that have been separated. In Exhibit 6.24, the opening bracket shows a *physical* separation of items. A Handling

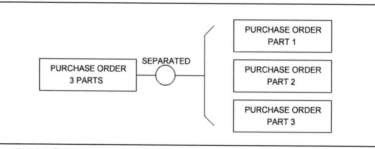

Exhibit 6.24 Separating Items

step represents the ungrouping activity and is placed directly before the opening bracket.

Logical Grouping.   Brackets are also used to logically group items that will be handled differently as a group along different alternative paths. Exhibit 6.25 represents a case for using a logical grouping. There are alternative flows where multiple items will be processed differently along each alternative branch. Obviously, we are not going to physically assemble a hard copy document and a computer application screen. The Tax Documents and the Account Record screen are logically grouped with a closing bracket. An alternative follows the closing bracket directly, and each branch begins with an opening bracket to once again display each item in the group. There are no handling steps associated with the brackets in a logical grouping because the items are not actually physically assembled or separated. It is a technique for handling alternative processing for groups of items.

A logical grouping consists of a single closing bracket followed immediately by a decision point and alternative paths that all begin with an opening bracket. There are no steps between the closing bracket and the opening brackets.

Logical Ungrouping.   A pair of brackets may also be used simply to display multiple items that are being processed as a group. Exhibit 6.26 demonstrates a logical ungrouping. An opening bracket is followed directly by the labels for each of the individual items, and the labels are followed with a closing bracket, bringing them once again to a single flow line.

A logical ungrouping may be used to identify individual items that are traveling together in a project folder, an admissions package, or a docket folder, for example. This enables us to display, at any point in a process, the labels of items that have been combined on a single line. It is particularly useful on long charts where it would be difficult to trace back to the labels of the documents that are represented by the line.

Alternatives

Alternatives display alternative process flows for a single item. When a flow line reaches a point where the item will be processed differently based on information provided by the item, a *Decision Point* is placed on the line. A set of two or more alternative branches will radiate from the Decision Point. Each time a document gets to this point, a decision is made as to which path to follow. In Exhibit 6.27, the amount of each purchase order will determine which of the paths the purchase order will follow. The number of paths is determined by the number of flow options that exist in the process.

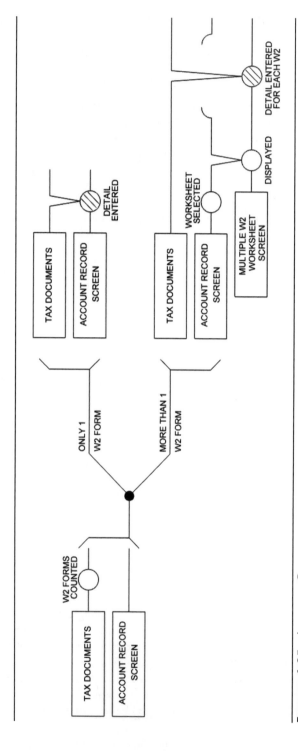

EXHIBIT 6.25 LOGICAL GROUPING

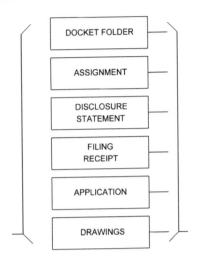

EXHIBIT 6.26 LOGICAL UNGROUPING

When the Decision Point does not involve inspection, it has the quality of sorting, and the symbol that precedes the Decision Point will be a Handling operation symbol. The words that accompany the Handling operation will describe some kind of sorting. In addition, there will be words that describe the sorting categories that may be written like an if statement (e.g., If over $100, If $100 or less). They appear next to the lines that radiate from the Decision Point, lines that can be thought of as tines of the "fork-in-the-road."

Typically, but not always, one path is the preferred path or the most common path. This path is referred to as the *main line* path and continues on the same line as the decision point.

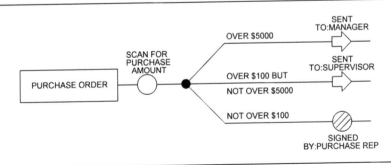

EXHIBIT 6.27 ALTERNATIVE PATHS

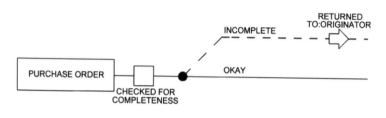

EXHIBIT 6.28 CORRECTION ROUTINE

Correction/Rejection

A Correction/Rejection convention (shown in Exhibit 6.28) is a variation of an alternate flow that describes what happens when an item fails an inspection. The symbol that precedes the Decision Point will be an Inspection symbol. The flow of an item that does not require correction or rejection is usually drawn straight ahead from the Decision Point, and a solid line is used. The flow of an item that requires correction or rejection is shown with a dotted line that branches up or down from the Decision Point. Words indicating the reason for the failure are placed at the beginning of each branch.

If the condition that caused the alternative flow is attended to and the items are treated alike thereafter, the flow lines will rejoin.

Rejoin

When a flow line has branched as a result of a decision, and the condition that caused the branching has been taken care of, the lines are brought back together with a Rejoin convention and are, once again, represented by a single line. Exhibit 6.29 shows three alternative paths. Two of the paths continue through different processing, then rejoin. Regardless of the different processing that occurred on the alternative paths, when the condition that caused the alternative processing is no longer valid or relevant, the paths are rejoined.

When the condition that causes an item to follow a correction path has been taken care of, the dotted line is brought back into the main line flow with a Rejoin. Exhibit 6.30 shows a correction routine rejoining a main line flow.

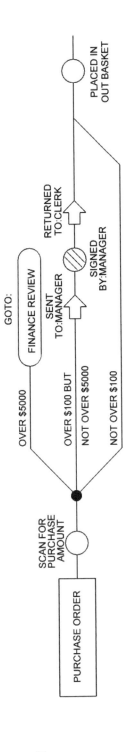

EXHIBIT 6.29 REJOIN OF ALTERNATIVE PATHS

61

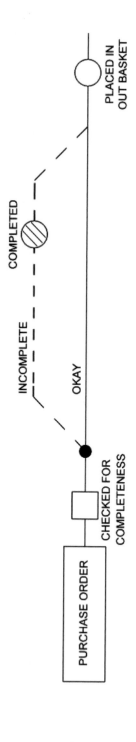

EXHIBIT 6.30 REJOIN OF CORRECTION ROUTINE AND MAIN LINE PATH

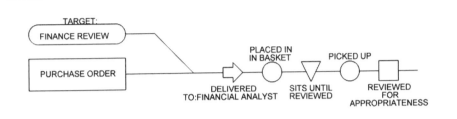

EXHIBIT 6.31 JOINING THE FLOW THROUGH A CONNECTOR

A Rejoin is also used to show a line joining a flow through a Connector label (see Exhibit 6.31). A Target connector represents an entry point that ties in from a Go-to connector on another chart or from another position on the same chart.

Connector Labels: Chart Links

Connector labels are used to show the continuation of a flow line on a different chart or at a different position within a chart. A Connector label is placed at the end of the terminated flow line and at the entry point where the flow is continued. The Connector label that is used at the end of a flow line is called a Go-to connector and identifies linkage to further processing at another location.

The Connector label that is used at the entry point in a flow line is called a Target connector *and* indicates linkage from another location. The Connector label that is placed at the entry point is tied into the existing flow line with a Rejoin.

Links may exist between separate charts or between locations within a single chart.

Connecting with Another Chart. When a flow line is terminated on one chart and continued on another chart, a Go-to connector appears at the point where the flow line stops. A target name and the file name of the chart where the flow continues are written in the Go-to connector. Exhibit 6.32 shows a segment of a process

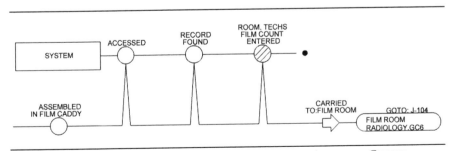

EXHIBIT 6.32 GO-TO CONNECTOR: CONNECTING TO ANOTHER CHART

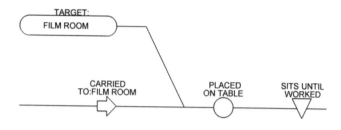

EXHIBIT 6.33 TARGET CONNECTOR: A CONNECTION FROM ANOTHER CHART

(a process for performing an ultrasound) that ends with a Go-to connector. The connector identifies the name of the chart where the process continues (RADIOL-OGY.GC6), a target name (FILM ROOM), and the grid location of the Target connector in the other chart (J-104).

A Target connector is used at the beginning of a line that joins into a flow in the second chart with a Rejoin, indicating a link from the previous processing on another chart. The Target connector may join another flow directly after the label that identifies the item or it may join anywhere along the process line. A target name is entered in the Target connector. Exhibit 6.33 shows the chart segment where the ultrasound process continues. The Target connector is labeled with the target name (FILM ROOM).

Rework. When an item is reprocessed through a series of steps that have already been completed, Go-to and Target connector labels are used within the same chart. The Go-to connector is placed in the flow line at the point where the processing stops and the item is being sent back for reprocessing (usually at the end of a Correction routine branch). The Target connector is joined back into the flow with a dotted rejoin at the point where reprocessing begins. Exhibit 6.34 shows a process segment where an AFE has been completed by an engineer and forwarded via e-mail to a district manager. When the district manager finds a problem with the AFE, a call is made to the engineer, who corrects the problem and re-signs and submits the form. At this point, the process flow loops back to the position in the chart where the engineer originally submitted the form.

Batch Work and Iterative Processing.   While a process chart typically represents the flows of individual items, some items may be processed as part of a batch. Where the chart displays only the individual item, batch processing is simply represented with a Delay symbol for the individual item while it waits for the rest of the batch to be processed. Where the chart displays an entire batch, a pair of connectors can be used, as with the rework scenario, to demonstrate the repeated processing. Exhibit 6.35 shows a simplistic document-scanning process segment.

The same applies to iterative work where a series of steps may be repeated a few times. An alternative path is placed following the series of steps. If another iteration is needed, the alternative connects back to a target connector at a position that reenters the flow line at the beginning of the series of steps. The item continues through this loop as many times as needed, then continues with the process by following the main line alternative path. Exhibit 6.36 shows an abbreviated segment of an admission process for a home-care patient. In this segment of the process, related parties are added to the patient's record. The process flows through this small loop until all related parties have been added.

Skipping Forward within a Chart.   Connector labels can also be used to show where a flow line skips a portion of a process. The Go-to connector is placed at the point in the flow line where the processing stops (usually at the end of an Alternative branch). The Target connector rejoins the flow line at the point where processing is continued.

Stop/Start

A Stop/Start convention is used to indicate a portion of the flow that is intentionally omitted. This may be a portion of the process that has flowed outside of the scope of the project or outside of the area of control. Or it may be a subprocess that has been charted separately. In any case, there is processing detail that has been intentionally left out of the process chart. Exhibit 6.37 shows a segment of a tax-processing chart. The Stop/Start refers to a letter process that is referred to in several of the tax processes. The letter process is a 24-step process to generate a letter to a taxpayer. Rather than repeating these steps each time they occur in a chart, the process was charted once and is referenced (with a Stop/Start or a Go-to connector label) wherever a letter would be printed. A Stop/Start is used in situations where processing continues after the subprocess is completed. If the subprocess occurs at the end of a process, it is referenced with a Go-to connector rather than a Stop/Start convention.

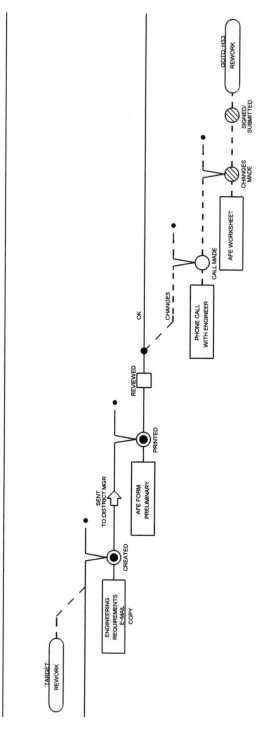

EXHIBIT 6.34 CONNECTOR LABELS SHOWING REWORK LOOP

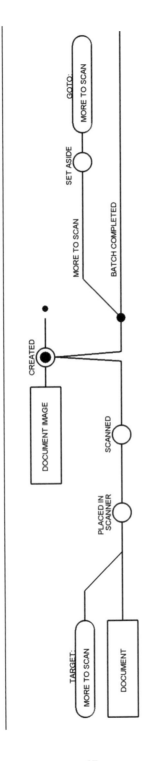

EXHIBIT 6.35 CONNECTOR LABELS: A BATCH PROCESSING LOOP

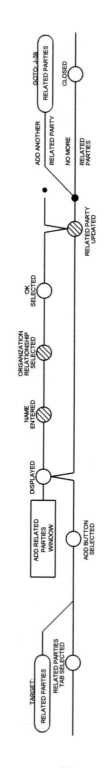

EXHIBIT 6.36 CONNECTOR LABELS: AN ITERATIVE PROCESS LOOP

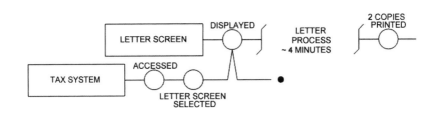

EXHIBIT 6.37   STOP/START CONVENTION

Words describing the omitted portion of the flow are placed inside the Stop/Start convention. Often the time typically required for the omitted portion of the process is included in the description.

Period

A period is placed at the end of a flow line that has been charted as far as the charter intends to chart it. Most flow lines end with a period. The period signifies completion and tells the charter and the reader that the flow line is intentionally ended at that point. The period is particularly useful to the charter in a long chart with many items. The charter knows that any line that ends with a period is completed, and if there is not a period (or a Destroy symbol or a Go-to connector label that also represents the end of a flow line), then the flow line has not been completed. Exhibit 6.38 shows the flows of three e-mails. The top line is used to verify a Real

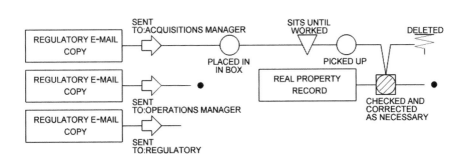

EXHIBIT 6.38   THE PERIOD

Property record, then the flow line is ended with a Destroy symbol. The real property record flow is terminated with a period. The middle e-mail is sent to the operations manager, then the flow line is terminated with a period. The bottom e-mail is sent to regulatory, then the flow line stops but is not terminated, indicating that that process line has not been completed. It is unfinished. Either a period or more steps and a period are needed.

Bypass

The *Bypass* convention is used to show that crossing lines are not related. When a horizontal flow line crosses an effect, a bracket, or a diagonal line of an Alternative, Correction, or Rejoin, the Bypass is used to avoid ambiguity. The horizontal line appears to jump over the vertical lines and indicates that it has nothing to do with them. Exhibit 6.39 shows a section of a medical admissions process where several documents provide data that are entered into a patient database. Most charters who have developed good charting skills try to arrange related documents next to one another to avoid bypasses; however, when three or more lines are repeatedly related, it may be inevitable that lines will cross.

Summary

This concise and effective set of symbols and conventions has enabled people to visualize and understand business processes for over half a century, providing a level of transparency that has contributed to billions of dollars in process improvement. It is a remarkably powerful and necessary process-charting methodology—because it is fundamental, because it speaks the language of process at a level of detail that makes clear just what steps of work are performed on each of the items in a process. Exhibit 6.40 is a section of a process that demonstrates the usage of all of the symbols and conventions.

WORDS: MAKING THE CHARTS TALK

The label is the subject and the symbols are verbs—the actions.

The process chart speaks the language of process. A person familiar with symbols and conventions can "read" a process flow that has no text. They can see the relationships between items, see where items are created, and see where other items are introduced to the process. They can see movement between work areas, delays, and value-added steps. Exhibit 6.41 shows an item that is created and transported to another work area. It is then placed somewhere, where it sits until it is picked up and updated. Information on the item is then used to pull or access another item and update that item.

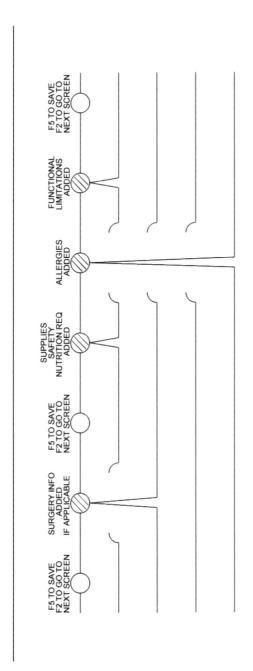

EXHIBIT 6.39 BYPASS CONVENTION

71

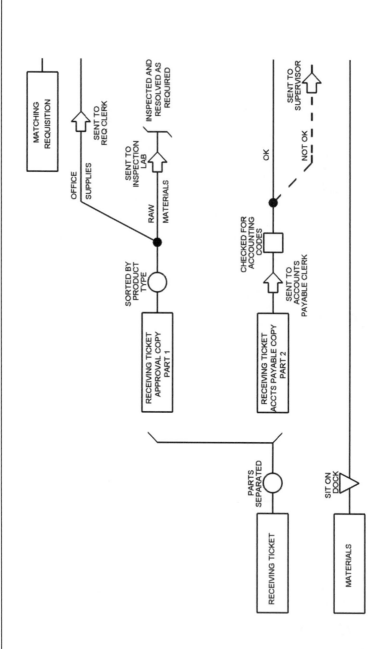

EXHIBIT 6.40 ALL THE SYMBOLS AND CONVENTIONS

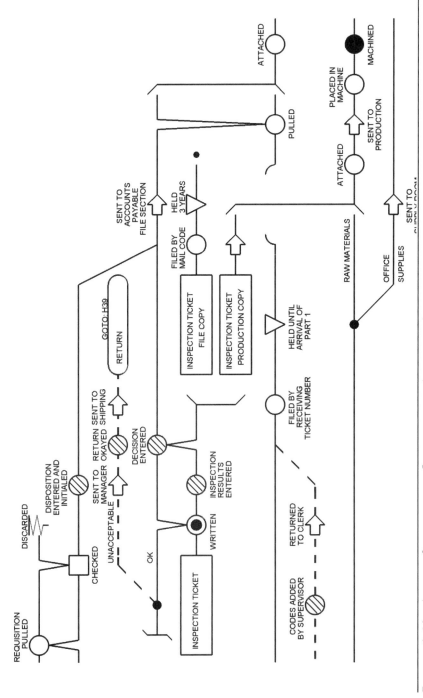

EXHIBIT 6.40 ALL THE SYMBOLS AND CONVENTIONS (*CONTINUED*)

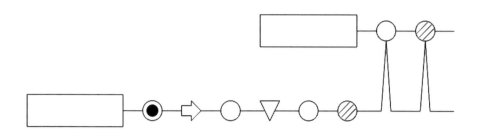

EXHIBIT 6.41   MAKING CHARTS TALK: LABELS AND SYMBOLS

Of course, this is just to demonstrate the inherent sensibility of the tool. However, it is obviously incomplete. But, all we need to do is add a few words of plain language text to each label, symbol, and alternative branch, and *anybody* can read it!

Labels identify each flow line. When the flow lines are identified as shown in Exhibit 6.42, we have a noun for every line. We know that every action along that line is occurring to the item identified by the label for that line.

It is a purchasing requisition that is prepared and taken somewhere where it sits. Information is added to the requisition, which is then used to access and update the purchasing system.

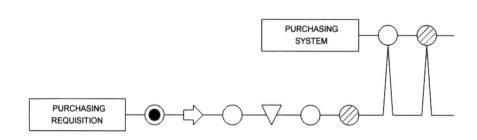

EXHIBIT 6.42   MAKING CHARTS TALK: IDENTIFYING THE ITEMS

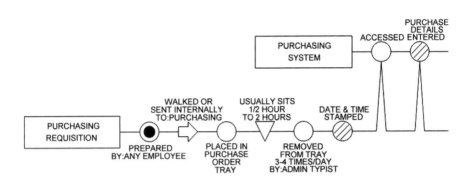

EXHIBIT 6.43   MAKING CHARTS TALK: THE LANGUAGE OF PROCESS

In Exhibit 6.43, a few words are associated with each step and the process is clear. For each step, the label and symbol text are combined to make a rudimentary sentence: A purchase requisition is prepared by any employee. The requisition is walked or sent internally to purchasing. The requisition is placed in the purchase order tray. The item name isn't repeated at each step because it doesn't need to be. The reader simply refers back to the label to be assured of what item a step is addressing.

Choosing the Right Words

The purpose of a process chart is to reflect reality. With just a few words associated with each symbol, the reader can understand what is happening, where the work is occurring, who is doing the work, and how long it takes to complete. The right words are presented by answering a few basic questions. Basic journalism classes teach that to write a complete story you need to answer a specific set of questions. The questions are often expressed in an order that seems to roll off the tongue naturally—who, what, when, where, why, and how. These are the same questions that are used in defining and analyzing business processes, but they are not treated equally. In defining a process (developing the as-is chart), the most important question to answer is, "What is happening?" The next set of questions is also important: "Who does the work? Where is it done? And when is it done?" Detail as to how the work is done is not as important. The question of why any step is performed should be avoided during data collection.

What? Identify what is happening at each step. The symbol by itself identifies the activity in general terms. A word or two is usually enough to complete a description of what is happening at each step. Words that are frequently used on process charts that answer the question, "What?" include: filled in, printed, copied, entered, signed, data added, sorted, filed, attached, merged, accessed, checked, verified, proofread, held, waits, delivered, carried, and so on. There are a few other things we will want to know.

Where? Identify where the work is being done at the first step, then whenever the workplace changes. These places in the process are easy to identify—the workplace changes at the transport symbols!

Who? Identify who does the work whenever someone new is introduced to the process. This will be at the first step if there is a person involved at that step and then whenever a different person picks up the work.

When? We can plainly see when one step occurs in relation to other steps because the steps are laid out in sequence. So when we provide information to clarify the question, "When?" we are really answering, "When will we move on to the next step?" We can approach this two ways: by identifying *when* a step will be completed or *how long* it will take to complete. If you answer the question, "When?" at the delays and at any other steps that take a significant amount of time, you will have documented most of the processing time.

When?	How Long?
Sits until 8:00 a.m. on Tuesday	Waits about 3 hours
Held overnight	Sits 15 to 45 minutes
Waits for acknowledgment letter	Held indefinitely

How? You might address how occasionally with a word or two, but it is not necessary to explore this question in detail. The label identifies the item and often tells us whether it is electronic, paper, or some other media that provides us with a little understanding of how the work is done. Leave the detailed explanation of how the action steps are completed to the people who will be analyzing the chart, and don't clutter your charts with discourse that simply can't compare to the detail inside the heads of the people who do the work.

Why?   Don't ask why! When you are preparing an as-is chart, it doesn't matter *why* people do what they do and, in fact, they may not know why they do what they are doing. "Why?" is different from the other questions in that it is evaluative. We should not be evaluating during fact gathering. It is premature. Asking why is apt to put people on the defensive, and it injects a sense of judgment or even criticism into the fact gathering. Save "why?" for analysis.

7

CHARTING BUSINESS PROCESSES

Always bear in mind that the purposes of any chart are (1) to help gather, organize or visualize the facts; (2) to aid in analyzing them; (3) to help in developing the better method and evaluating it; (4) to assist in convincing management of the improvement's value.

—Ben S. Graham

Detail process charts may include 20, 200, or 2,000 steps. A relatively simple process will likely fall into the range of 50 to 150 steps. For larger charts, it is common practice to break them into more manageable parts (100 to 200 steps), although all the parts will be worked with during analysis. As even a small chart is difficult to present in a book-page format, the examples presented in this book represent short processes or sections of larger processes. These chart segments are presented with the symbols and conventions spaced tightly together for the sole purpose of getting more on a page. On actual charts, the symbols and conventions are spaced further apart. Examples of complete charts prepared with proper spacing are shown at the end of some of the scenarios.

A number of scenarios of different process situations are provided here. These examples represent specific types of organizations, but they should not suggest that these are the industries in which detailed charts apply. They apply in and have been used in every imaginable type of organization and at all levels within those organizations. They are explained with a brief (but thorough) narrative to simulate what a person would observe when collecting the data. Each scenario sets up the boundaries of the process to be charted. The purpose of the process is identified, and start and end points are provided. If you had actually collected the data, you would be armed with much more knowledge than we could possibly capture in a short narrative. You would have pictures in your mind of the person actually doing the work and of the workplace. You would also have a number of forms and screen prints at your disposal. Accept for the moment that these limited presentations represent reality and you will see how quickly they can be transformed into process charts that any reasonable person can read and understand.

CHARTING PROCESS SCENARIOS

This chapter presents four process scenarios. The first two are explained in great detail to get you started. It is important to work with these first. The later examples are explained with less detail, but they are increasingly more complicated. Special situations that can be difficult to visualize are covered at the end of this chapter.

1. Paying for gas with a credit card
   - Paying at the pump
   - Paying at the counter
2. Charting an online auction bid
   - Charting multiple screens along a single path
   - Charting multiple screens displayed as separate lines
3. Processing a purchase requisition
4. Processing police officer overtime

Paying for Gas with a Credit Card

Here are two simple examples that are included because most people can visualize the steps of buying gas clearly. The objective is to document two scenarios for purchasing gas with a credit card. In the first scenario, the transaction occurs at the pump. In the second scenario, the transaction occurs in an office after the gas is pumped. The main item to be charted is the credit card, but the chart will also include items supporting the credit card payment process. The starting point will be when the vehicle arrives at the pump, and the end point will be when the vehicle leaves the pump. The chart will document the credit card transaction only and will not include the vehicle, gas, or person(s) involved in the process.

Paying at the Pump.   With a clipboard in hand, the charter follows the credit card through the process.

The vehicle pulls up to the pump. The credit card is in the driver's wallet. The driver (with the credit card) gets out of the vehicle and walks to the pump. The credit card is removed from the wallet by the driver and inserted into the credit card reader on the pump. The reader reads the credit card detail and verifies that the card is in good standing. It then ejects the card, which is removed by the driver and is replaced in the wallet. The credit card sits in the wallet while the gas is pumped. After the gas is pumped, a receipt is printed. The receipt is removed from the printer and placed in the wallet (along with the credit card). The driver gets back in the vehicle and drives away.

Exhibit 7.1 represents the notes that would be captured during observation, including the shorthand (symbols) in the right columns. The main difference between this presentation and actual notes is that these include more complete sentences and are more legible than rough notes. This layout is similar to the Flow Process Chart developed by Frank Gilbreth that has been used so successfully throughout the past century.

Collecting facts that represent reality is a more demanding task than it appears to be. It requires practice and discipline. Facts should be observed at the workplace.The

OBSERVATION	Credit Card	Other Items
The vehicle pulls up to the pump. The credit card is in the driver's wallet.	▽	
The driver (with the credit card) gets out of the vehicle and walks over to the pump.	⇨	
The credit card is removed from the wallet by the driver.	◯	
The credit card is inserted by the driver into the credit card reader on the pump.	◯	
The reader is updated with the credit card detail.		⊘
The credit card is verified by the card reader.	▢	
The credit card is ejected from the reader and removed by the driver.	◯	
The credit card is replaced in the driver's wallet.	◯	
The credit card sits in the wallet while the gas is pumped.	▽	
After the gas is pumped, a receipt is printed.		◉
The receipt is removed from the printer.		◯
The receipt is placed in the wallet (with the credit card).		◯
The driver gets back in the vehicle and drives away.	⇨	

EXHIBIT 7.1   GAS PURCHASE: PAY AT THE PUMP PROCESS NOTES—TEXT AND SYMBOLS

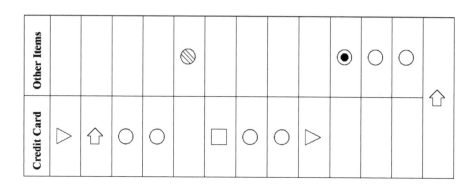

EXHIBIT 7.2   GAS PURCHASE: CONVERTING NOTES TO A CHART

good news is, once the facts have been collected, converting them to a chart is relatively easy! Turn your shorthand notes sideways so that the credit card and other item headings are in the first column on the left (see Exhibit 7.2) and you're halfway there!

Every item in a process chart is identified with a label. A label is placed at the beginning of every flow line. This chart begins with a label that identifies the credit card (see Exhibit 7.3).

A line extends to the right from the Credit Card label. The line represents the flow, the passage of time as the credit card passes through the several activities that make up the gas purchase process. Symbols are placed along the line, left to right, in the order they occur. The symbols represent each of the actions (the things that happen to the credit card). A period placed at the end of the flow indicates that the chart has been intentionally ended. Exhibit 7.4 shows only the flow of the credit card.

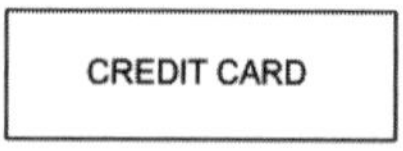

```
┌─────────────────┐
│   CREDIT CARD   │
└─────────────────┘
```

EXHIBIT 7.3   GAS PURCHASE: EVERY LINE BEGINS WITH A LABEL

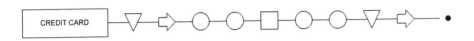

EXHIBIT 7.4   GAS PURCHASE: FLOW WITHOUT TEXT

In Exhibit 7.5, a few descriptive words added to each step, above or below the symbol, complete the process flow for the credit card. It is written in plain language that can be read and understood by just about anyone.

This process also includes other items that would normally be introduced into the chart as they are encountered in the process. Exhibit 7.6 shows the flow of the credit card and how it ties to other items in the process. This chart is spaced properly to make it easier to read. It would be about two feet long if were printed out at a more legible working size.

Following the step where the card is inserted into the card reader, the reader is introduced as a new line beginning with its label. It is tied to the credit card with an effect pointing from the card to the reader that shows the credit card providing information to the reader. The next effect, which points from the reader to the card, shows the reader (system) verifying the card. The reader reads the information that the card provided and compares it against a database to see if the card is valid. The next effect is between the reader and the receipt (another label and line) where the reader is printing out the receipt. The final tie in this short process is the closing bracket that shows the receipt being placed with the credit card in the wallet. All three items are tied together to produce a detailed chart of the credit card "Pay at the Pump" process.

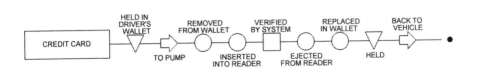

EXHIBIT 7.5   GAS PURCHASE: SINGLE ITEM FLOW

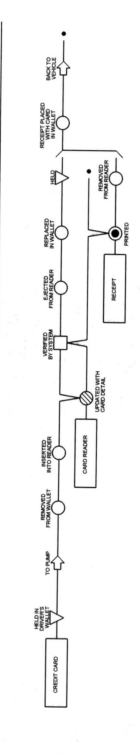

Exhibit 7.6 Gas Purchase: "Pay at the Pump" Process

Paying at the Counter.   With a clipboard in hand, the charter once again follows the credit card through the process.

The vehicle pulls up to the pump. The credit card is in the driver's wallet. The driver gets out of the vehicle and walks over to the pump. The card continues to sit in the driver's wallet while the gas is pumped. After the gas is pumped, the driver walks to the office and removes the credit card from the wallet. The driver hands the card to the station clerk who swipes it through a reader. The credit card is verified by the card reader. The card is placed with a purchase slip on an imprinter and an imprint of the card is made on a purchase slip. The card is handed back to the driver who places it back in the wallet. The purchase slip is filled in by the clerk and then handed to the driver for signature. The driver signs the purchase slip, removes the customer copy, and hands the establishment copy back to the clerk. The driver places the customer copy of the purchase slip in the wallet, returns to the vehicle, and drives away.

Exhibit 7.7 represents the notes that would be captured during observation.

Exhibit 7.8 shows the first nine steps of the "Pay at the Counter" process. The chart begins with a label that identifies the item and symbols are placed, left to right, in the order they occur along a horizontal line that extends from the label.

When a second item, the purchase slip, is introduced in the process, a second label is drawn and a second line is begun, as shown in Exhibit 7.9. The credit card line (below the purchase slip line) provides cardholder information to the purchase slip (the card number and detail that is imprinted on the slip), so there is an effect from the Credit Card line into an origination symbol on the Purchase Slip line. The number of gallons and price are provided by the gas pump register at the counter and written on the purchase slip by the clerk. Once the credit card information is captured, the card is returned to the driver and placed back in the wallet, and the purchase slip is handed to the driver for signature.

In Exhibit 7.10, the purchase slip is separated into two parts, so the Purchase Slip flow line is separated into two lines (with an opening bracket), and both lines start with a label. The labels no longer just identify the purchase slip, but identify the specific parts of the purchase slip (establishment copy and customer copy). The customer copy is placed with the credit card (the bottom line) in the wallet (with a closing bracket). The credit card and purchase slip are then transported back to the vehicle together as a single line.

Exhibit 7.11 shows the "Pay at the Counter" process (properly spaced to make it easier to read). This is a short process with only 19 steps. Yet, if this chart were printed at a reasonable working size, it would be two to three feet long.

OBSERVATION	Credit Card	Other Items
The vehicle pulls up to the pump. The credit card is in the driver's wallet.	▽	
The driver gets out of the vehicle and walks over to the pump.	⇨	
The card continues to sit in the wallet while the gas is pumped.	▽	
After the gas is pumped, the driver walks to the office.	⇨	
The driver removes the credit card from the wallet.	◯	
The driver hands the card over to the station clerk.	◯	
The card is swiped through a reader by the clerk.	◯	
The credit card is verified by the card reader.	☐	
The card is placed with a purchase slip on an imprinter.	◯	
An imprint of the card is made on the purchase slip.		⊙
The card is handed back to the driver.	◯	
The driver replaces the credit card in the wallet. The purchase slip is filled in by the clerk.	◯	⊘
The purchase slip is handed to the driver for signature.		◯
The driver signs the purchase slip.		⊘
The driver removes the customer copy of the purchase slip.		◯
The driver hands the establishment copy back to the clerk.		◯
The driver places the customer copy of the purchase slip in the wallet.		◯
The driver returns to the vehicle and drives away.	⇨	

EXHIBIT 7.7   GAS PURCHASE: "PAY AT THE COUNTER" PROCESS NOTES—TEXT AND SYMBOLS

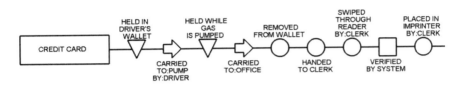

EXHIBIT 7.8 GAS PURCHASE: CREDIT CARD FLOW

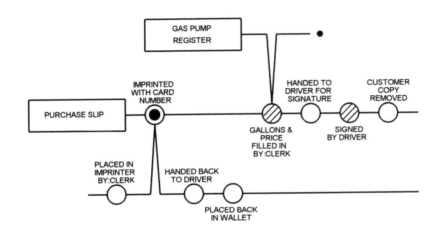

EXHIBIT 7.9 GAS PURCHASE: PREPARING A PURCHASE SLIP

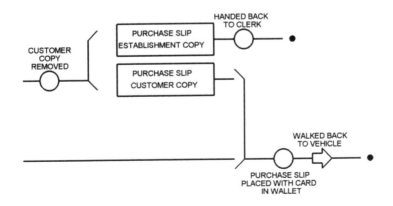

EXHIBIT 7.10 GAS PURCHASE: COMPLETING THE CREDIT CARD TRANSACTION

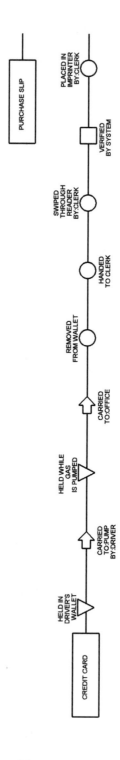

PURCHASE SLIP

PLACED IN
IMPRINTER
BY CLERK

VERIFIED
BY SYSTEM

SWIPED
THROUGH
READER
BY CLERK

HANDED
TO CLERK

REMOVED
FROM WALLET

CARRIED
TO OFFICE

HELD WHILE
GAS
IS PUMPED

CARRIED
TO PUMP
BY DRIVER

HELD IN
DRIVER'S
WALLET

CREDIT CARD

EXHIBIT 7.11 GAS PURCHASE: "PAY AT THE COUNTER" PROCESS

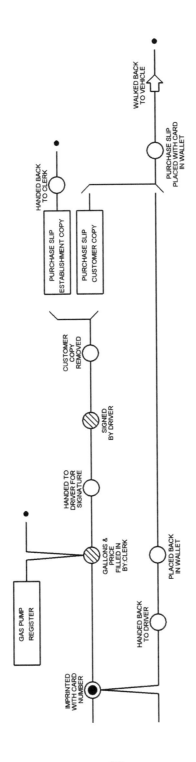

EXHIBIT 7.11 Gas Purchase: "Pay at the Counter" Process *(Continued)*

Charting an Online Auction Bid

All of the steps in the online auction example are electronic. The project objective may call for displaying each screen in an electronic application as a separate item, or all screens may be identified in steps along a single line. Displaying each screen as a separate line provides system information for detailed analysis, but it also makes the chart more confusing to read. If there is no opportunity to change the system or if the purpose of the chart is to provide an overall understanding of the process, concentrating on the people interfaces, then displaying the application as a single-line approach may be adequate. If the single-line approach is taken, it can always be expanded when the project calls for it. In this example, the flow of the activity is presented first as a single-line flow and then with the detail of each screen (Web page) displayed.

The process begins at the point where the bidder launches an Internet browser and continues through the viewing of and bidding on online auction items until the bidder leaves the auction site and closes the browser. The actions are traced of a bidder visiting an online auction site and keying in search criteria (names of things to bid on). A list of items that match the search criteria is displayed and the bidder has an opportunity to click on any item to display more information about that item. After reviewing the detail page about an item, the bidder may elect to bid on that item. The bidder may decide to place a bid on an item and enter a bid amount. The system will compare the bid with the highest existing bid, then display a message telling the bidder the new high bid and whether the bidder is the high bidder or has been outbid by another person. The chart will capture bid and no-bid conditions.

With a clipboard in hand, follow the process, beginning with the bidder accessing the Internet, by launching an Internet browser.

Charting Multiple Screens along a Single Path.   Since all of the steps in the auction process occur on different pages of the Internet, a single flow line represents the Internet. The pages that are accessed throughout the process are represented as steps along the Internet flow line. Exhibit 7.12 shows the Internet being accessed with the launch of the browser. The auction site Web address is entered and the auction site is displayed in the browser. The bidder enters search criteria to locate specific items to bid on.

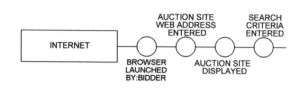

EXHIBIT 7.12   ONLINE AUCTION: ACCESSING THE AUCTION SITE

Notice that all the steps in Exhibit 7.12 are Handling operations. (*Note:* The text is alternating above and below the symbols only for convenience in spacing. The location of the text does not have any process significance.) You may wonder why it is shown as Handling when information is entered. The information that is entered is not actually changing information on the Internet; it is simply used to perform a lookup. The bidder is not adding new information but is looking to see if what was entered is already there. Compare it to finding the right file cabinet, opening the right drawer, and thumbing through the folder tabs to find a specific folder. When searching electronically, we can often get to our objective directly by using some sort of search function. If the bidder visits the auction site regularly, the address might even be listed someplace where it can be selected from a menu.

As a result of the search, a list is displayed of the items that matched the search criteria. The bidder looks through the items and makes a choice. Three alternatives are shown in Exhibit 7.13. If there is nothing of interest, the bidder may decide to end the process by closing the browser. If there is nothing of interest in this list, the bidder may decide to continue searching by entering new search criteria. In the case where new criteria are entered, Connector labels show the process looping back on the chart to reenter at the point where the search results list is displayed. Finally, the bidder may see an item of interest and select that item to pursue it further. When the bidder double-clicks on an item, another page is displayed that provides more detail about that item.

The bidder reads through the detail page, then makes a choice. Two alternatives are shown in Exhibit 7.14. If not interested, the bidder clicks the back button to return to the search results list. The Connector label links back on the chart to the "SEARCH" Target connector that reenters the flow at the point where the search results list is displayed, as it did in Exhibit 7.13. If the bidder is interested in the item, a bid amount is entered. Once the bid is entered, it is submitted by selecting the "Review Bid" button. The Bid page is displayed and the bidder enters a User ID and password. A click on the "Place Bid" button will display the Bid Results page.

The bid results are shown in Exhibit 7.15. This Bid Results page is displayed and shows the new high bid, along with two possible outcomes for the bidder. The bidder is either the new high bidder or has been outbid by another bidder. In either case, as the next step, the bidder clicks the back button and returns to the Bid page. In the case where the bidder has entered the high bid, the next two steps are to back up to the item list to continue bidding on other items or quit. (The bidder can actually quit just about anywhere in the process. The chart shows the quitting step in a logical place to represent a normal process.) If outbid, the bidder can either choose to enter a new bid or may simply back up to the item list to search for another item.

To increase the bid amount, the bidder clicks the back button to return to the item page where a new bid can be entered. This time the connector is linked to the "BID" Target connector that reenters the process where the item detail page is displayed, as shown previously in Exhibit 7.13. The complete process is shown in Exhibit 7.16.

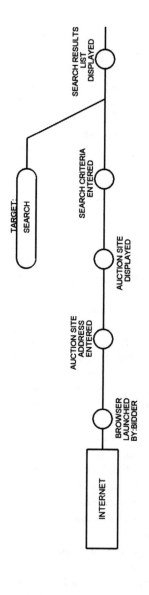

EXHIBIT 7.13 ONLINE AUCTION: FINDING AN ITEM

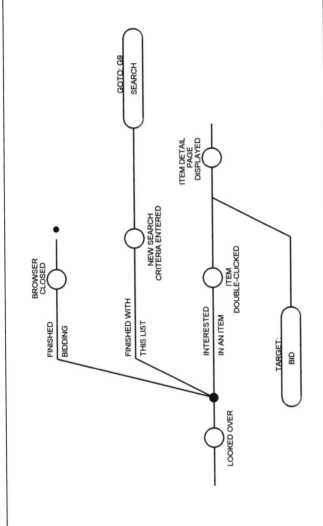

EXHIBIT 7.13 ONLINE AUCTION: FINDING AN ITEM (*CONTINUED*)

93

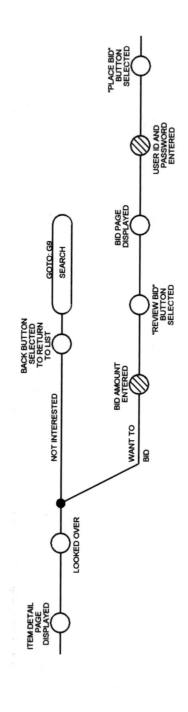

EXHIBIT 7.14 ONLINE AUCTION: PLACING A BID

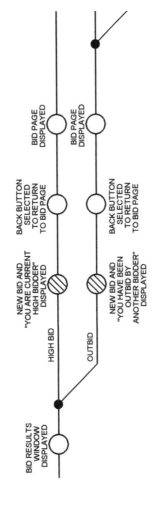

BID RESULTS
WINDOW
DISPLAYED

HIGH BID

OUTBID

NEW BID AND
"YOU ARE CURRENT
HIGH BIDDER"
DISPLAYED

NEW BID AND
"YOU HAVE BEEN
OUTBID BY
ANOTHER BIDDER"
DISPLAYED

BACK BUTTON
SELECTED
TO RETURN
TO BID PAGE

BACK BUTTON
SELECTED
TO RETURN
TO BID PAGE

BID PAGE
DISPLAYED

BID PAGE
DISPLAYED

EXHIBIT 7.15 ONLINE AUCTION: BID RESULTS

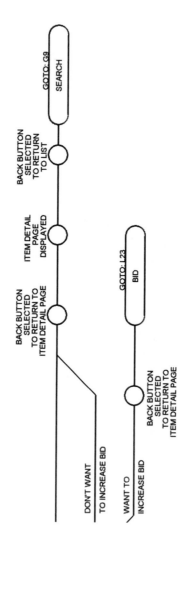

EXHIBIT 7.15 ONLINE AUCTION: BID RESULTS *(CONTINUED)*

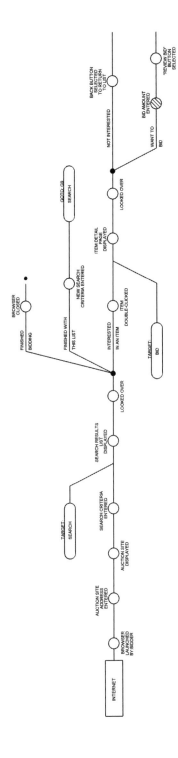

INTERNET

BROWSER
LAUNCHED
BY BIDDER

AUCTION SITE
ADDRESS
ENTERED

AUCTION SITE
DISPLAYED

SEARCH CRITERIA
ENTERED

TARGET:
SEARCH

SEARCH RESULTS
LIST
DISPLAYED

LOOKED OVER

FINISHED
BIDDING

FINISHED WITH
THIS LIST

INTERESTED
IN AN ITEM

BROWSER
CLOSED

NEW SEARCH
CRITERIA ENTERED

ITEM
DOUBLE-CLICKED

TARGET:
BID

GOTO-OB:
SEARCH

ITEM DETAIL
PAGE
DISPLAYED

LOOKED OVER

NOT INTERESTED

WANT TO
BID

BID AMOUNT
ENTERED

BACK BUTTON
SELECTED
TO RETURN
TO LIST

"REVIEW BID"
BUTTON
SELECTED

EXHIBIT 7.16   ONLINE AUCTION: COMPLETE SINGLE-PATH FLOW

97

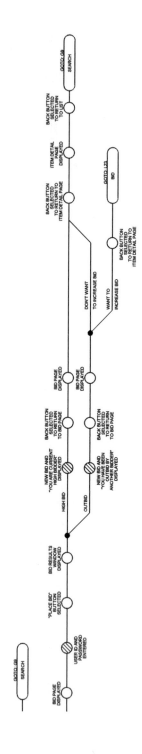

Exhibit 7.16 Online Auction: Complete Single-Path Flow *(continued)*

Charting Multiple Screens Displayed as Separate Lines. Each Web page
that is accessed in this representation of the auction process is represented with its
own process line. Exhibit 7.17 shows the launch of the Web browser. The auction
site Web address is entered into the browser to display the auction site. The bidder
enters search criteria into the auction site page to locate specific items to bid on.

As a result of the search, a list is displayed of the items that matched the search
criteria. The bidder looks through the items and then makes a choice. Three alternatives are shown in Exhibit 7.18. If there is nothing of interest, the bidder may
decide to end the process by closing the browser. If there is nothing of interest in
this list, the bidder may decide to continue searching by entering new search criteria. In the case where new criteria are entered, Connector labels show the process
looping back on the chart to reenter at the point where the search results list is displayed. Finally, the bidder may see an item of interest and select that item to pursue it further. When the bidder double-clicks on an item, another page is displayed
that provides more detail about that item.

The bidder reads through the detail page, then makes a choice. Two alternative
paths are shown in Exhibit 7.19. If not interested, the bidder clicks the back button
to return to the search results list. (The chart connects back to the search results list
as shown in Exhibit 7.20.) If the bidder is interested in the item, a bid amount is
entered. Once the bid is entered, it is submitted by selecting the "Review Bid" button. The Bid page is displayed and the bidder enters a User ID and password. A
click on the "Place Bid" button will display the Bid Results page.

In Exhibit 7.19, if not interested, the bidder clicks the back button to return to the
search results list. Continuing along that path in Exhibit 7.20 (the top line), there are
no more symbols and the line ends with a Connector label. The Connector label links
back on the chart to the "SEARCH" Target connector that reenters the flow at the
point where the search results list is displayed, as it was shown in Exhibit 7.18. The
bid results are shown in the bottom part of the chart in Exhibit 7.20. The Bid Results
page shows the new high bid along with two possible outcomes for the bidder. The
bidder is either the new high bidder or has been outbid by another bidder. In either

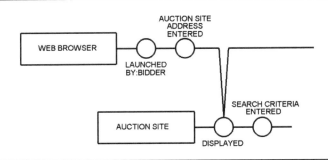

EXHIBIT 7.17   ONLINE AUCTION: ACCESSING THE AUCTION SITE

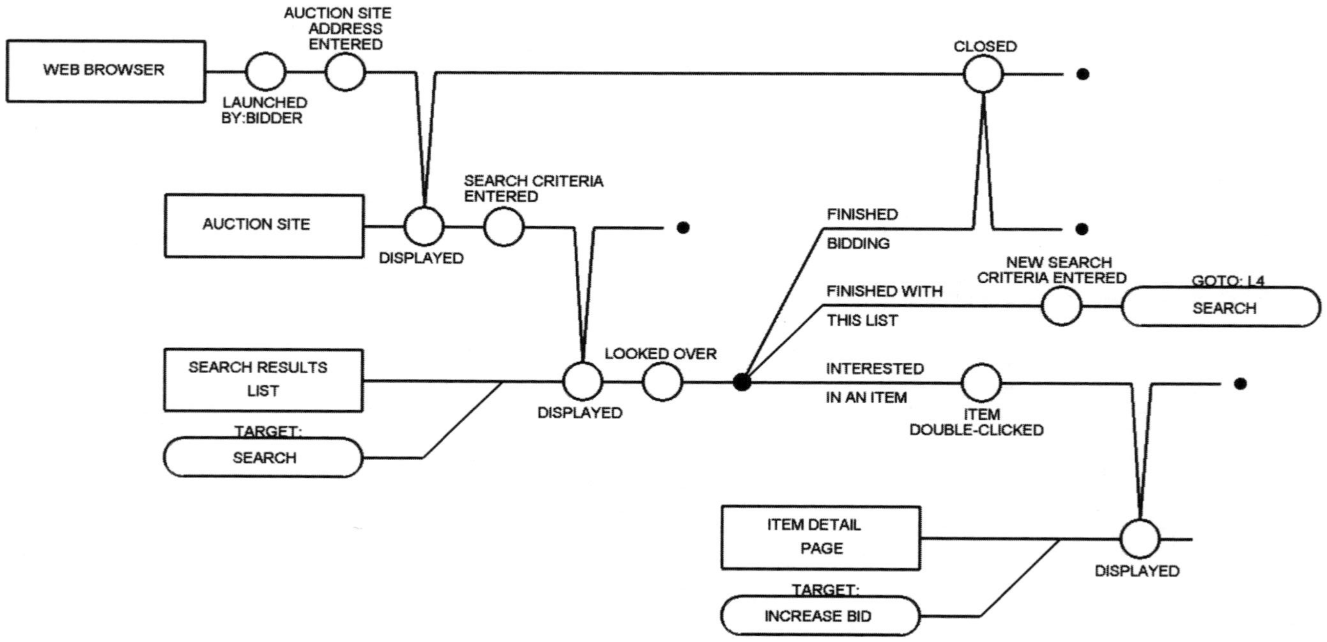

EXHIBIT 7.18 ONLINE AUCTION: FINDING AN ITEM

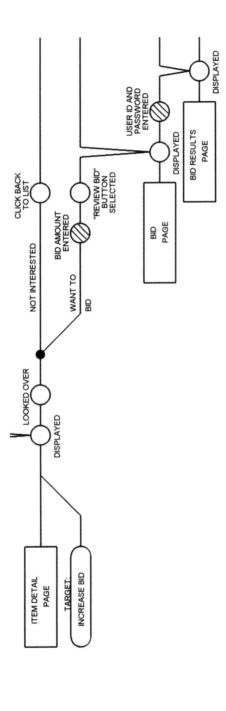

EXHIBIT 7.19 ONLINE AUCTION: PLACING A BID

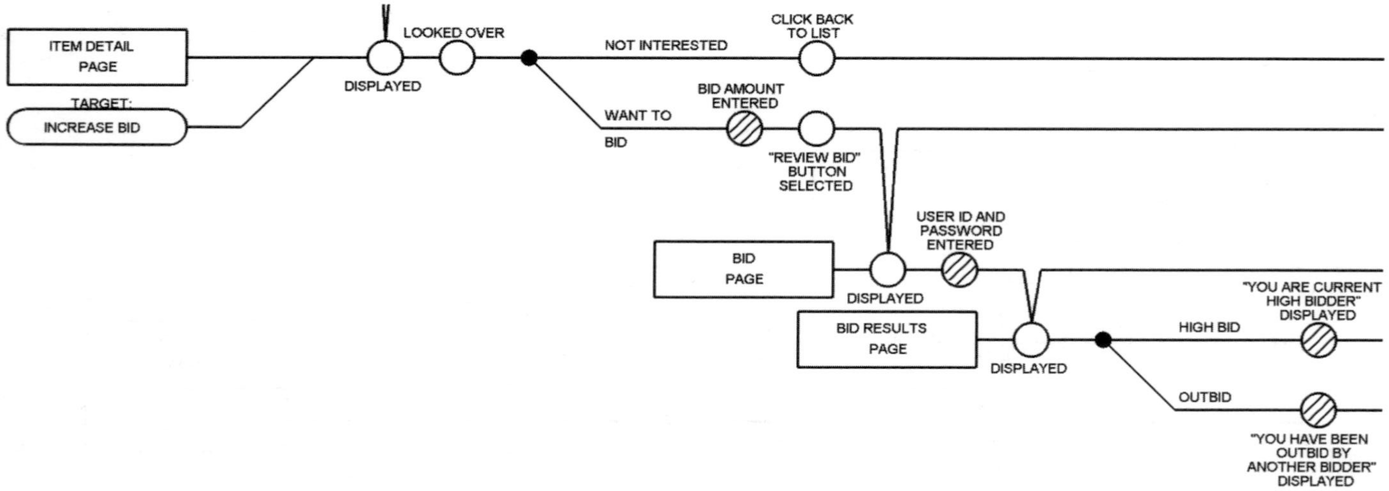

EXHIBIT 7.20 ONLINE AUCTION: BID RESULTS

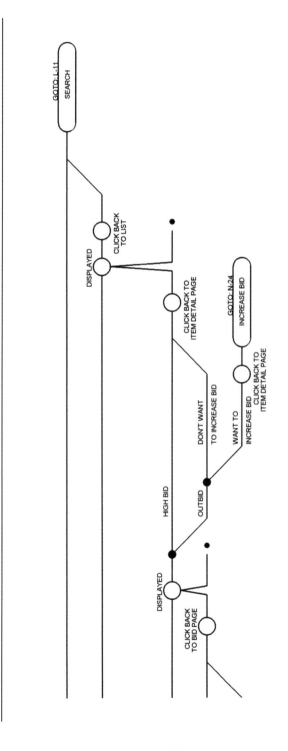

EXHIBIT 7.20 ONLINE AUCTION: BID RESULTS *(CONTINUED)*

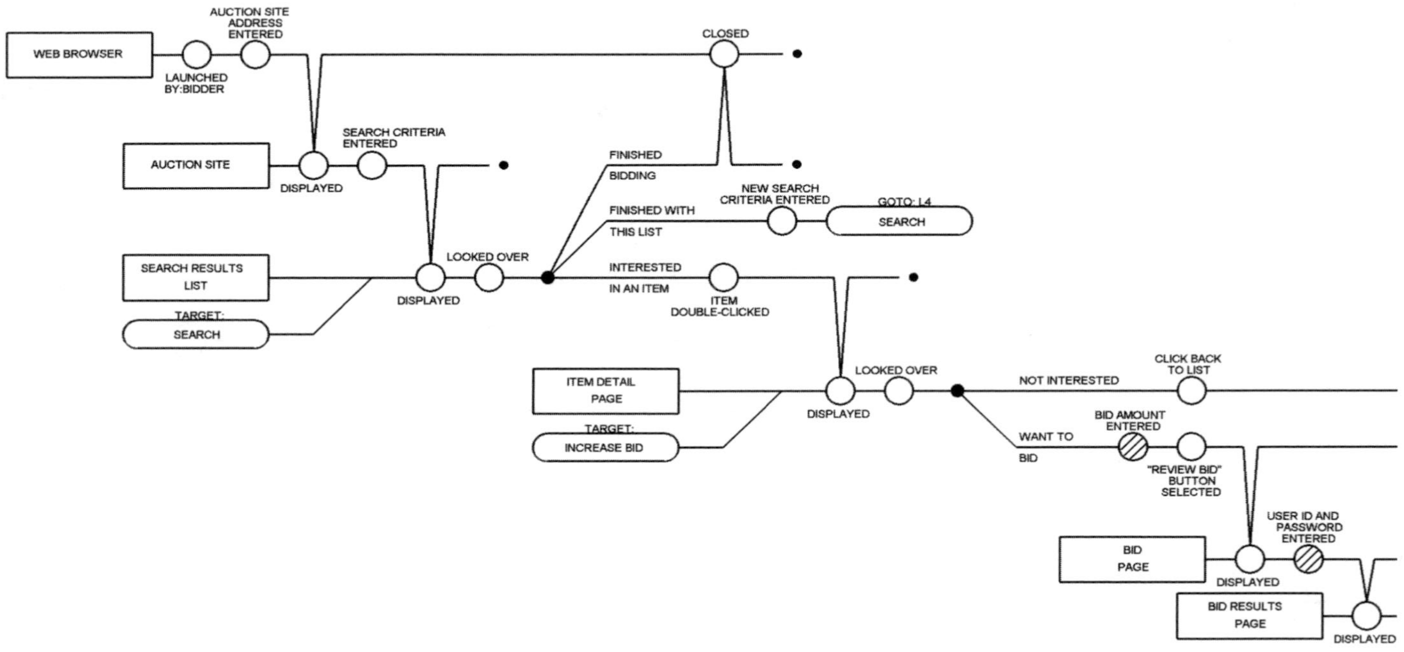

EXHIBIT 7.21 ONLINE AUCTION: COMPLETE MULTIPATH FLOW

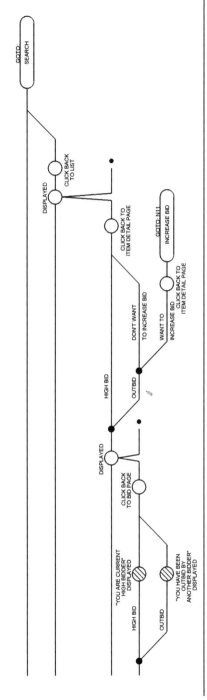

EXHIBIT 7.21 ONLINE AUCTION: COMPLETE MULTIPATH FLOW *(CONTINUED)*

105

case, as the next step, the bidder clicks the back button and returns to the Bid page. In the case where the bidder has entered the high bid, the next steps are to back up to the item list to continue bidding on other items or quit. (The bidder can actually quit just about anywhere in the process. The chart shows the quitting step in a logical place to represent a normal process.) If outbid, the bidder can either choose to enter a new bid or may simply back up to the item list to search for another item.

To increase the bid amount, the bidder clicks the back button to return to the item page where a new bid can be entered. This time the connector is linked to the "INCREASE BID" Target connector that reenters the process at the point where a bid is entered. The complete process is shown in Exhibit 7.21.

Processing a Purchase Requisition

This requisitioning process involves preparing an online requisition from a quote, including one or more line items, then printing the requisition and forwarding it for approval. The quote is received from a vendor by an employee who wishes to make a purchase. The employee then forwards the quote to the requisitioner, who enters the purchase information into the purchasing system so the purchasing department can make the purchase. This process segment begins when a quote is received by the requisitioner and continues to the point where a hard copy of the requisition is forwarded to the department director for approval.

Exhibit 7.22 shows a quote in the requisitioner's inbox. The quote is looked over, then used to create a requisition in the purchasing system. Accounting and expense codes are entered on the requisition form. The requisitioner usually knows what these codes are but can refer to a budget code list if there is a question. The requisition is saved and line item detail is selected.

The quote is used to enter the product details for one item at a time. After the item description and other details are entered, the data are saved. The chart shows a connector loop that is followed to enter multiple line items. The Go-to connector at the right end of the segment shown in Exhibit 7.23 loops back to the Target connector at

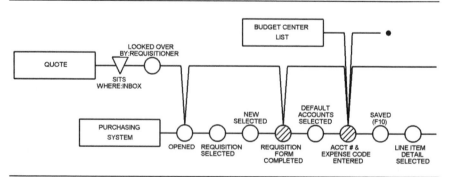

EXHIBIT 7.22   PURCHASE REQUISITION: CREATING THE ONLINE REQUISITION

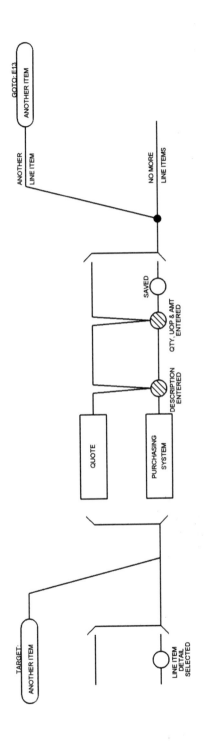

Exhibit 7.23 Purchase Requisition: Entering Line Items

the beginning of the segment. The Target connector rejoins a short line segment between closing and opening brackets. These brackets indicate a logical grouping and ungrouping of the quote and purchasing system. For each line item, the requisitioner will use the quote to update the purchasing system. The connectors represent a loopback of both the quote and the purchasing system.

Exhibit 7.24 shows the requisition being printed. After all the line items have been entered, the requisitioner selects print requisition to create an image file of the requisition. Since the quote and purchasing system were grouped to show the loopback alternative, they are ungrouped first. The requisition file is printed from the purchasing system as shown with the effect from the purchasing system line into the Origination symbol on the requisition file line. The requisition file is printed to produce a hard copy requisition, and the requisition number is transcribed from the hard copy requisition onto the quote. The system is updated to "pending approval" status and closed.

The bottom line in Exhibit 7.25 is the quote (the label is not visible in this chart segment). The quote is taken to the copier, where a copy is made. The original and the copy are taken back to the requisitioner's desk and separated. The copy is placed in an interoffice mailer and sent to the purchasing department. The original is stapled to the hard copy of the requisition and delivered to the director's office.

The entire purchase requisition process is displayed in Exhibit 7.26. A small chart with only 32 steps, it would extend four to five feet if printed as a legible working chart.

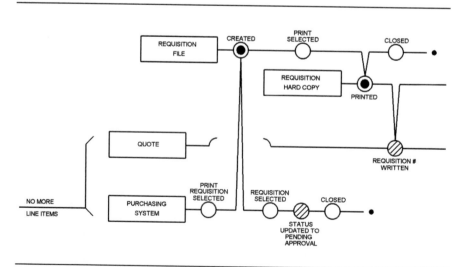

EXHIBIT 7.24   PURCHASE REQUISITION: PRINTING THE REQUISITION

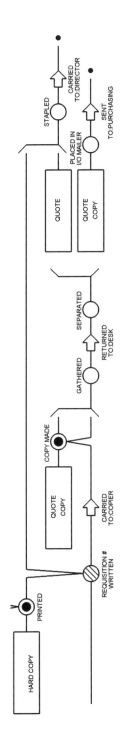

EXHIBIT 7.25 PURCHASE REQUISITION: FORWARDING HARD COPIES

Processing Police Officer Overtime

This is an example of part of an actual process before it was improved. If it seems somewhat convoluted or confusing, that is because it is. It includes alternative processing paths, grouping and separating forms, and multiple approval levels. Simply by preparing the process chart, the process is easier to understand *and* opportunities for improvement are apparent. This process segment documents the flow of an employee overtime slip from the time it is prepared to the point that it is delivered to the district superintendent. The overtime slip will pass through several approval levels and will include alternative processing flows depending on the nature of the overtime. The process will be observed with several different overtime slips in order to capture the alternative flows.

With a clipboard in hand, follow an overtime slip.

Exhibit 7.27 shows the beginning of this process. A three-part overtime slip is completed by an officer, who removes the pink copy and keeps it. When the pink copy is removed, there are two physically separate items (Parts one and two are still together and the pink copy has been detached). The physical separation activity is shown with a Handling symbol, followed directly by an opening bracket that shows the separation of a single line into two lines. (The symbol shows the action and the bracket separates the lines.) The opening bracket is followed directly by two labels that identify each of the separated items. The employee keeps the pink copy. This is as far as we intend to chart the pink copy, so the flow line is terminated with a period. Parts one and two will follow a path that is determined by the type of overtime work that was done.

Three situations require special processing. The others are processed normally. The special situations include work performed under contract, work performed under a grant, and court detail. Variations in processing are shown with a decision point and four alternative branches, as shown in Exhibit 7.28. Each branch will continue as a series of alternative processing steps along a different horizontal path.

Under normal circumstances, Parts one and two of the overtime slip are dropped off at the sergeant's desk. The sergeant will eventually review the slip. If it is okay, the sergeant will sign it and forward it to the commander's desk. If the overtime slip is incomplete or if it includes errors, the sergeant will identify the problem and return the slip to the officer to be corrected. Exhibit 7.29 follows the overtime slip along the normal processing branch.

In the case where the overtime slip is incomplete, a Connector label tells us that the slip goes back to the employee (officer), where it can be completed/corrected and reprocessed. Exhibit 7.30 takes us back to the beginning of the process. A Target connector and a short correction routine process are shown. The correction routine is identified with a dotted line. Once the corrective steps have been taken, the correction flow line rejoins the normal processing line. Since it is the overtime slip

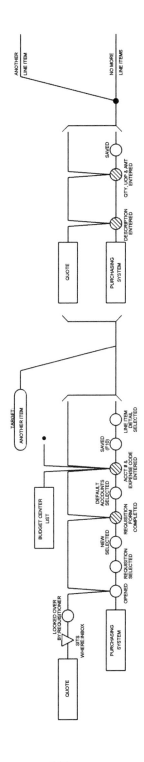

EXHIBIT 7.26 PURCHASE REQUISITION PROCESS

111

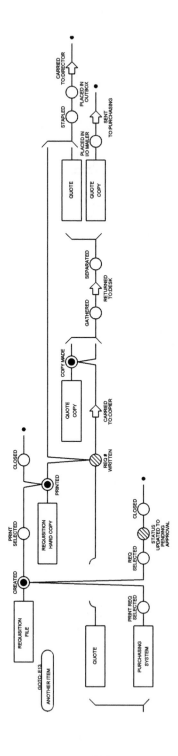

EXHIBIT 7.26 PURCHASE REQUISITION PROCESS *(CONTINUED)*

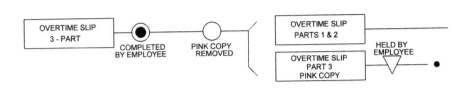

EXHIBIT 7.27 POLICE OFFICER OVERTIME SLIP

that is being sent back, it needs to rejoin the overtime slip line. It rejoins the normal processing flow line just before the step where the overtime slip is walked to the sergeant's desk.

Exhibit 7.31 shows that when the sergeant finds a problem with the overtime slip, six additional steps are introduced into the process (those on the dotted lines) and four steps are repeated. The processing cost of a mistake is 10 steps.

The district commander will eventually review the slip, as shown in Exhibit 7.32. If rework is required, the problem will be identified and the slip will be returned to the sergeant. If there are minor errors that can be corrected by the commander, they will simply be corrected and the overtime slip will continue along the normal processing path. The commander will sign the slip and place it in the assistant's inbox.

The assistant will eventually use the overtime slip to update an overtime log and a mail log and then place the overtime slip in the outbox to be picked up and delivered to the district superintendent as shown in Exhibit 7.33. This completes the normal processing branch of the process segment as it was defined in the scope.

If the overtime was performed under a grant (this is one of the alternative paths), the officer completes a three-part grant slip and staples it to the overtime slip as shown in Exhibit 7.34. Then the overtime slip with the attached grant slip is passed on to the sergeant and continues to follow the normal processing path, so the grant work line rejoins the normal processing line.

If the overtime was court detail, the completed overtime slip is handed over to the court detail clerk (or mailed to the court detail clerk about 5 percent of the time). In Exhibit 7.35, the court detail flow is shown along the bottom alternative path. The court detail clerk eventually codes the slip and reviews it. If the slip is incomplete or in error, the court detail clerk will identify the problem and return the slip to the officer to be corrected. If it is okay, it will be sorted along with other slips; first by major and then alphabetically. Then it is passed on to the court detail supervisor's office.

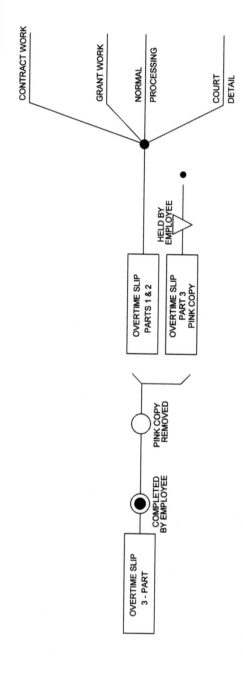

EXHIBIT 7.28 POLICE OVERTIME: ALTERNATIVE PROCESSING

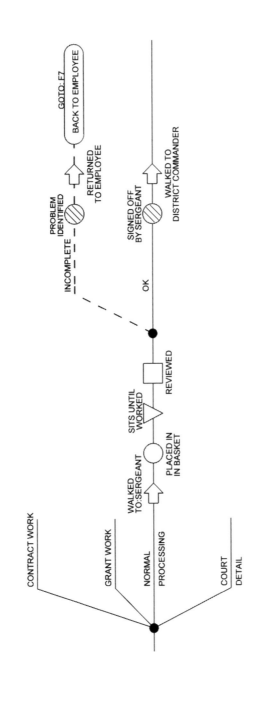

Exhibit 7.29 Police Overtime: Normal Processing

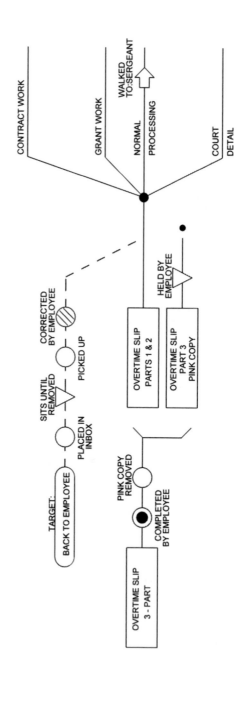

EXHIBIT 7.30 POLICE OVERTIME: CORRECTING A PROBLEM

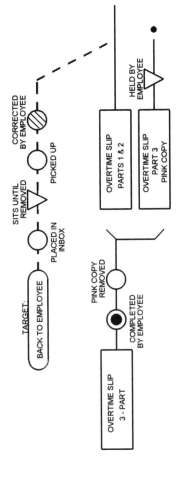

117

EXHIBIT 7.31 POLICE OVERTIME: CORRECTION ROUTINE

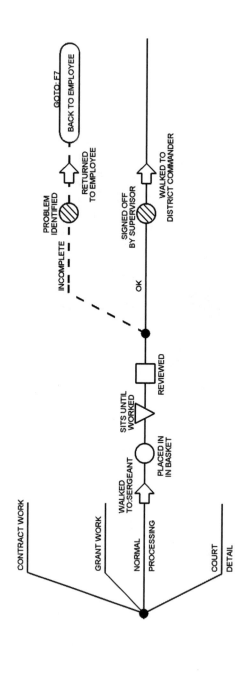

EXHIBIT 7.31 POLICE OVERTIME: CORRECTION ROUTINE *(CONTINUED)*

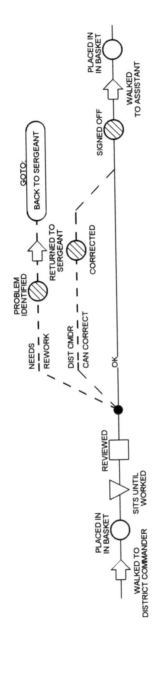

Exhibit 7.32 Police Overtime: Commander Review

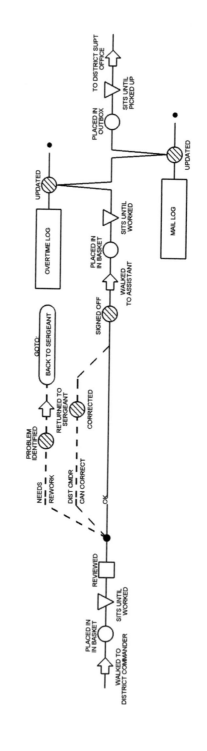

EXHIBIT 7.33 POLICE OVERTIME: LOG UPDATES

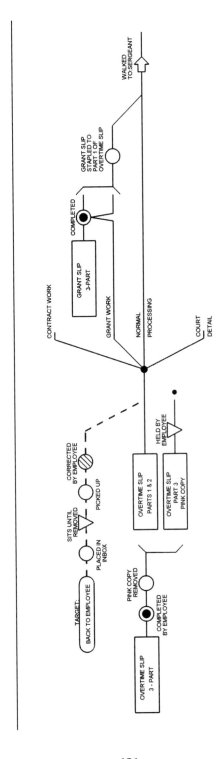

EXHIBIT 7.34 POLICE OVERTIME: GRANT WORK

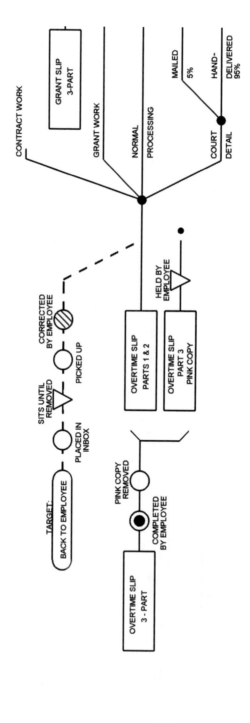

EXHIBIT 7.35 POLICE OVERTIME: COURT DETAIL PROCESS START

122

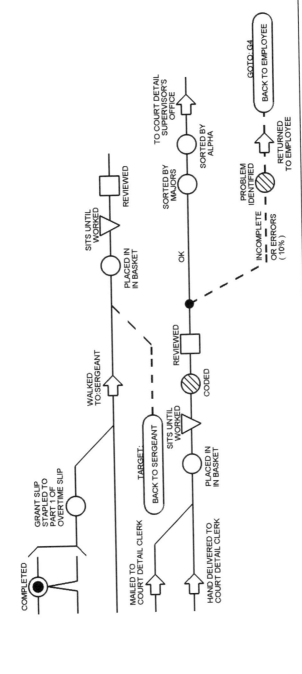

EXHIBIT 7.35 POLICE OVERTIME: COURT DETAIL PROCESS START *(CONTINUED)*

The court detail path continues as the bottom line in Exhibit 7.36, which shows that the court detail supervisor eventually reviews the overtime slip. It is usually signed, but if there is a problem, the court detail supervisor identifies the problem and sends it back to the officer to be corrected. If signed, it is forwarded to the district superintendent. From this point forward, the slip is processed normally, so the court detail line rejoins the normal processing line to follow the same path.

The remaining alternative path is for contract work. In Exhibit 7.37, along the top alternative path the officer completes a three-part contract service slip, removes the pink copy, and staples parts one and two of the contract services slip to part one of the overtime slip. The overtime slip is then forwarded to the contract coordinator's desk. The contract coordinator eventually codes the overtime slip and passes it on to a sergeant for sign-off. The sergeant eventually signs off and returns the slip to the contract coordinator.

The contract coordinator eventually separates the contract services slip from the overtime slip, removes part two of the contract services slip and places it in an out-box to the business manager, as shown along the top flow in Exhibit 7.38. The original contract services slip is restapled to the overtime slip and forwarded to the district superintendent. From this point forward, it is processed normally, so the contract work line rejoins the normal processing line to follow the same path.

Exhibit 7.39 shows the entire section of the police overtime process that was just worked through.

SPECIAL SITUATIONS

There are a few situations that can be difficult to visualize until you see them charted. These include the following scenarios:

- Using e-mail
- E-mailing multiple recipients
- Faxing and remote printing
- Processing batch work
- Charting multiple source items
- Creating multiple copies
- Sorting and distributing multiple document copies
- Including flow lines of people in process charts

Some of these situations are presented in the following discussion.

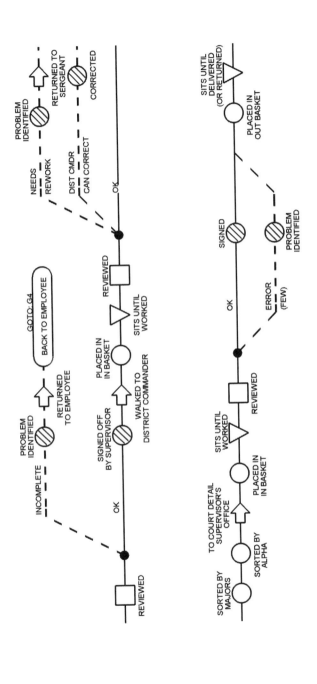

Exhibit 7.36 Police Overtime: Court Detail Completed

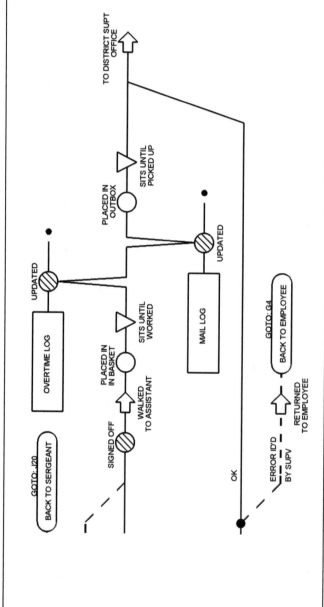

EXHIBIT 7.36 POLICE OVERTIME: COURT DETAIL COMPLETED *(CONTINUED)*

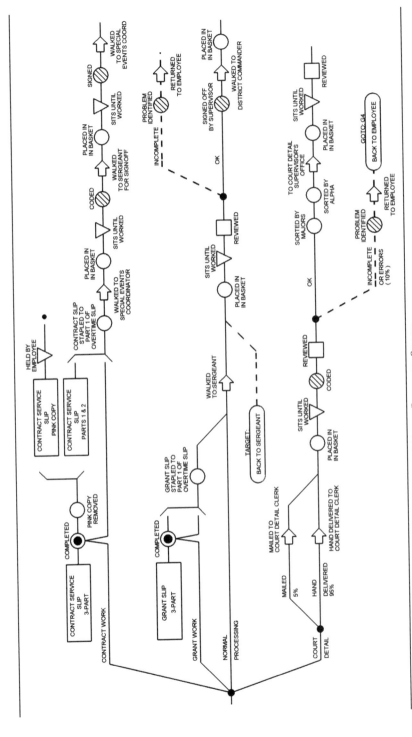

EXHIBIT 7.37 POLICE OVERTIME: CONTRACT WORK PROCESS START

127

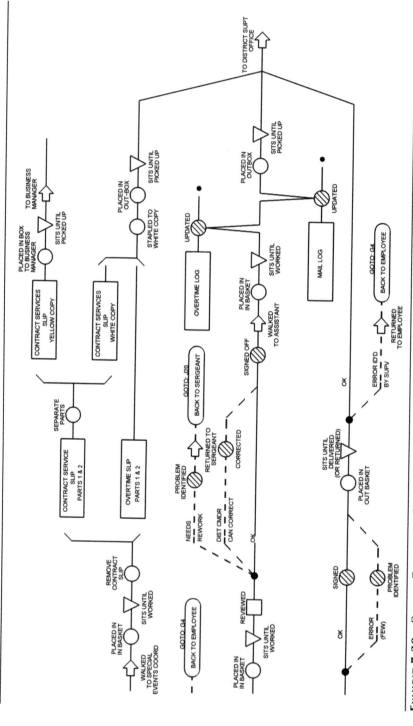

EXHIBIT 7.38 POLICE OVERTIME: CONTRACT WORK PROCESS END

128

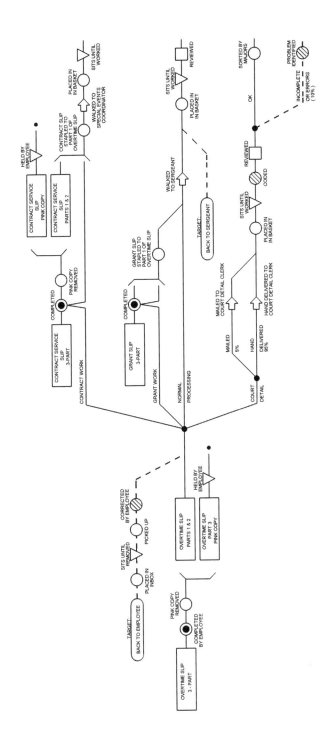

EXHIBIT 7.39 POLICE OVERTIME: COMPLETE PROCESS

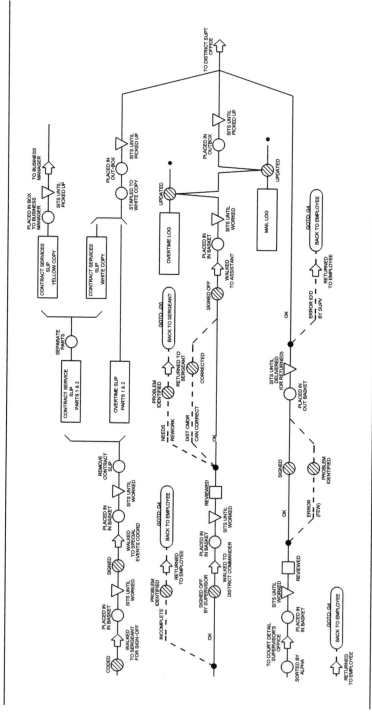

EXHIBIT 7.39 POLICE OVERTIME: COMPLETE PROCESS *(CONTINUED)*

Using E-Mail

Charting e-mail is similar to charting a hard copy document. An e-mail is prepared, then sent on to a recipient. In Exhibit 7.40, a research assistant writes an e-mail to a legal assistant to inform the legal assistant of the availability of an invention report on the legal server. The legal assistant reads the e-mail, locates the invention report on the legal server, opens the report, and prints it out.

Exhibit 7.41 shows a similar scenario; only this time the report is sent as an attachment. Notice that it is a copy of the invention report that is attached. The legal assistant opens the e-mail with the attachment, then opens and prints the attachment.

E-Mailing Multiple Recipients

Exhibit 7.42 shows an e-mail prepared with an attachment and sent to several recipients. The e-mail is prepared and a copy of the business case is attached. The attachment is identified as a copy and the e-mail is identified as e-mail. The text associated with the Origination symbol specifies five recipients, so five copies of the e-mail are sent. The five copies are represented by the five flow lines following the opening bracket.

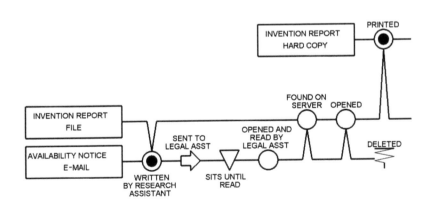

EXHIBIT 7.40 CHARTING E-MAIL

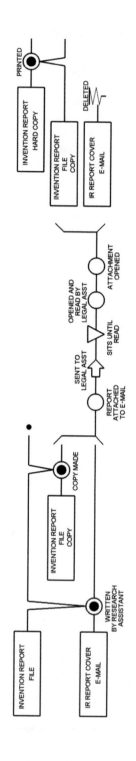

EXHIBIT 7.41 CHARTING E-MAIL WITH AN ATTACHMENT

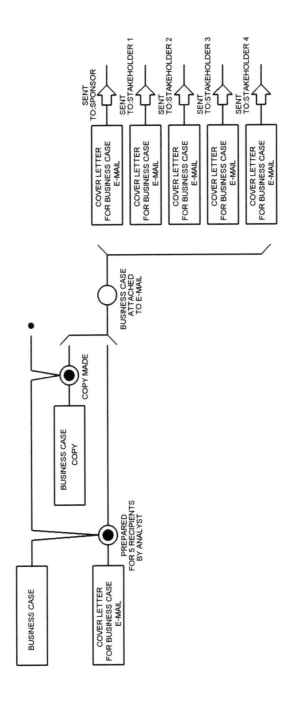

EXHIBIT 7.42 CHARTING E-MAIL WITH MULTIPLE RECIPIENTS

It is common practice for the sender to retain a copy of e-mail sent. In Exhibit 7.43, the top flow line following the opening bracket represents a copy of the e-mail that is retained by the sender.

Faxing and Remote Printing

Sending faxes and printing remotely involve the creation of a new document at a different location. We chart documents and files but not the electric transmission of data. It is easy to ensure that the chart is complete and that the reader will see that the document is printed at another location simply by identifying the location at the origination symbol.

Faxed documents are created at a different location, as it is not normal practice to send a fax to your own workstation. (I worked with an organization where clerks routinely used a department fax to send document images to themselves so they could distribute them via e-mail—they were using the fax as a scanner.) The label identifies the new document as a fax, and the location of the fax is clarified by identifying it with the first step for that document, the Origination symbol. The chart segment in Exhibit 7.44 shows a request form for certified copies of patent papers being faxed from the legal department in an organization to the Patent and Trademark Office.

The chart segment in Exhibit 7.45 is part of an order process at an office equipment reseller. It shows an order being printed by a person at a satellite warehouse. The order is printed at the central distribution center. With remote printing, the location where the document is printed is identified at the first symbol for the printed document, the Origination symbol.

Processing Batch Work

Process flow lines represent the flow of individual items through a process. An item that is processed as part of a batch can be easily demonstrated in a chart. An important aspect of batch processing is the processing time. While individual items may take minutes or seconds to process, if they are being processed as part of a batch there will necessarily be delay time while the rest of the batch is being processed.

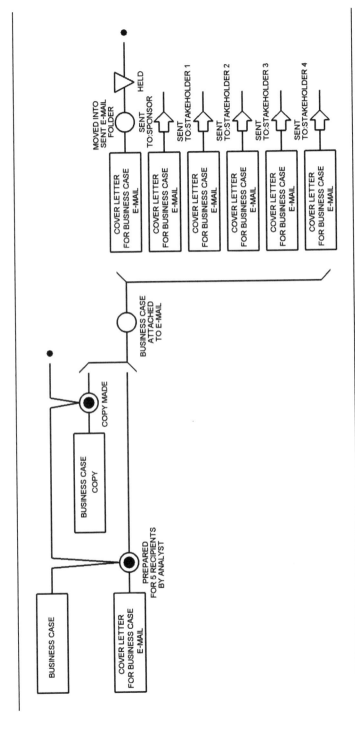

EXHIBIT 7.43 CHARTING E-MAIL: KEEPING A COPY

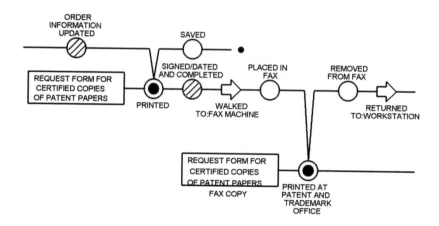

EXHIBIT 7.44   SENDING A FAX

Individual items may be grouped together with a closing bracket to travel through a process as a batch. Still, the value-added steps, inspections, and much of the handling of batches typically address each item one at a time. For instance, a chart that reflects a batch of orders being used to update a purchasing system represents *each order* traveling through the process individually, typically with gathering and sorting steps that associate the individual item with a batch.

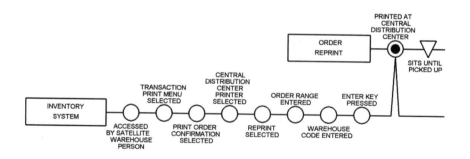

EXHIBIT 7.45   REMOTE PRINTING

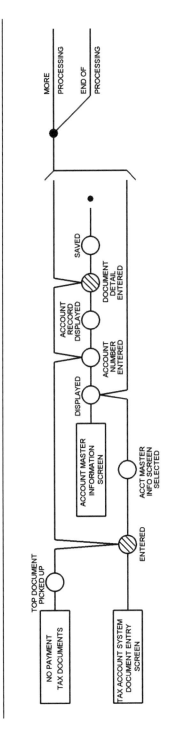

EXHIBIT 7.46 BATCH PROCESSING: ONE BY ONE

The process segment in Exhibit 7.46 shows a batch of local tax documents being entered into a government tax account system. The batch of documents is being processed by a clerk, who picks up the document on top of the batch and processes it.

If there are more documents to process, as shown in the top path in Exhibit 7.47, the document that was just completed is set aside, where it waits for the rest of the batch to be processed. When all the documents have been processed (shown in the bottom path of Exhibit 7.47), they are assembled and moved on to the supervisor as a batch.

As long as there are more documents to be worked, the process loops back to repeat the same steps for the next document. The loop back is displayed in Exhibit 7.48 with Connector labels at each end of the chart segment. Items are received as a batch, worked individually, and then set aside to accumulate (delay time) in a batch.

Charting Multiple Source Items

Sometimes several source documents (items) are used to create a new item. There are a few different ways to present multiple items affecting a single item. The relationship between two items is shown with an effect. When there are multiple source items affecting one new item, an effect is used for each relationship. The simplest way to document this situation is presented in Exhibit 7.49. Each of the three source items has an effect pointing into the Origination symbol on the new item.

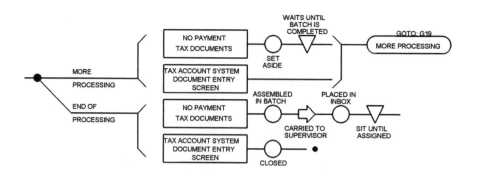

EXHIBIT 7.47   BATCH PROCESSING: ACCUMULATING A BATCH

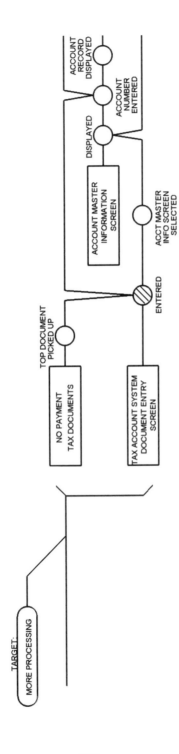

EXHIBIT 7.48 BATCH PROCESSING

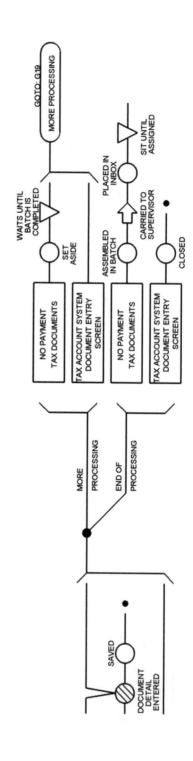

EXHIBIT 7.48 BATCH PROCESSING *(CONTINUED)*

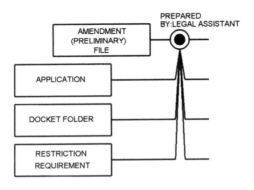

EXHIBIT 7.49   MULTIPLE SOURCE DOCUMENTS

In some cases, the source items may have been collected together as a single item. We can still show the individual items that make up the source, as demonstrated in Exhibit 7.50.

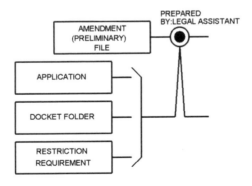

EXHIBIT 7.50   MULTIPLE SOURCE DOCUMENTS: GROUPED

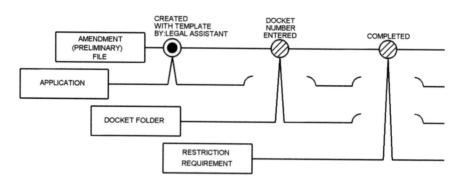

EXHIBIT 7.51   MULTIPLE SOURCE DOCUMENTS: SEQUENCED

In Exhibit 7.51, three source documents are used sequentially. The charter wants to capture that sequence in the chart and specific information from one of the documents.

Creating Multiple Copies

Creating a copy involves the introduction of a new item line. When there are multiple copies, the number of copies is identified in the Origination symbol text. In Exhibit 7.52, the Origination symbol represents six new copies of an inspection notice. The six copies are gathered up with the original and returned to the workstation.

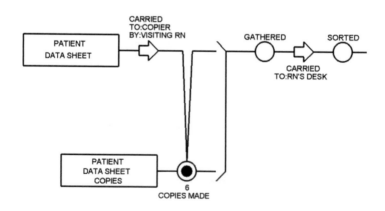

EXHIBIT 7.52   CREATING MULTIPLE COPIES

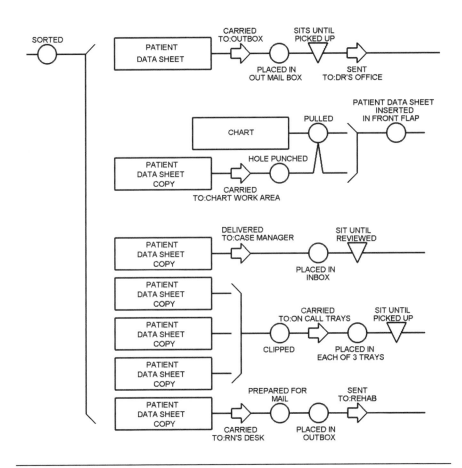

Exhibit 7.53 Sorting and Distributing Multiple Copies of a Single Document

At the workstation, the documents are sorted and distributed as shown in Exhibit 7.53.

Sorting and Distributing Multiple Document Copies

Exhibit 7.54 demonstrates a situation where there are several copies of more than one document that are sorted and distributed. In this process segment, a counter clerk has three plan sets, a card, and a permit application. Three copies of the application are made, and then the clerk sorts them to associate the original application and two of the copies each with a plan set.

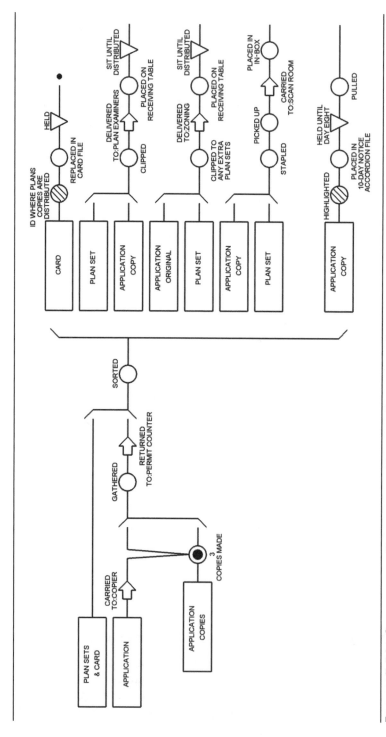

EXHIBIT 7.54 SORTING AND DISTRIBUTING MULTIPLE DOCUMENT COPIES

Including Flow Lines of People in Process Charts

Detail process charts systematically identify who is doing the work wherever a person is involved in a process. In most cases, people are not charted as items in order to keep the focus of the chart *on the process*. However, there are situations where it makes sense to chart people. An operating person may be charted when there is a particular concern with a particular aspect of the process. For example, a mail delivery person may be charted where there is a concern with travel, a person working in a vault or mint may be charted where there is a concern with security, and a nuclear plant worker may be charted where there is a concern with safety. In these cases, simply follow the path of the person being charted and tie them into the chart along with the documents, forms, files, and so on.

An example of a different type of situation that logically calls for a person to be charted is when the work or part of the work to be processed is a person (e.g., a patient in a hospital admissions process, a prisoner in a booking process, a new employee in a hiring process). These types of processes can be charted without charting the person being processed. *However*, charting the flow of the person can bring to light customer service issues concerning delays, excessive traveling between processing areas, security and control issues, and so on. Here again, simply follow the path of the person being charted.

A third type of situation that calls for charting people is where a process includes a *verbal exchange of information*. This situation is probably as difficult to conceptualize (from a process standpoint) as anything we chart. The reason is that the information is captured and stored in a brain and transmitted *invisibly* without the aid of a pen or a keystroke.

It will help to remember that a chart shows the flow of physical items (including electronic documents, paper documents, and people). An information transaction is shown on the chart as a value-added step along the flow line of a physical item.

Typically, we show the transfer of information from a person's brain to a document/form by identifying the person in the text associated with the step they performed. In Exhibit 7.55, a Customer prepares an *order*.

A person can also provide information verbally that is captured on a physical or electronic document/form by a different person. In Exhibit 7.56, the transmission of information is shown as an effect from the *Customer* line to the *Order* line. The *customer* is providing information that triggers the creation of an *order* by the order clerk. The *customer* has only provided information.

EXHIBIT 7.55   CHARTING PEOPLE: CUSTOMER PREPARES AN ORDER

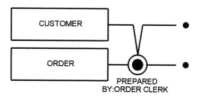

EXHIBIT 7.56 CHARTING PEOPLE: CUSTOMER PROVIDES INFORMATION IN PERSON

When the request is transmitted over a phone, the chart is nearly the same. The transmission of information is shown as an effect from the *Customer Phone Call* line to the *Order* line. The *Customer Phone Call* (the customer on the phone) is providing information that triggers the creation of an *Order* by the order clerk. In Exhibit 7.57, again, the *customer* has only provided information.

This illustration demonstrates that even though the customer and order clerk are in different locations, there is no transportation step involved. The customer and the order are charted, neither of which have moved.

We don't chart the verbal transmission of information, but rather the recording of information; then the handling, updating, reviewing, and moving of the recorded information.

Exhibit 7.58 shows a process segment in a telecommunications environment where it may be advantageous to capture detail related to the phone call (answering, transferring, putting on hold, and so on).

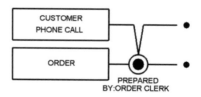

EXHIBIT 7.57 CHARTING PEOPLE: CUSTOMER PROVIDES INFORMATION OVER THE PHONE

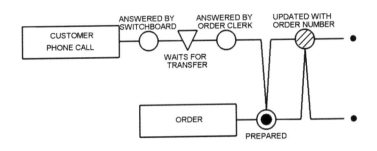

EXHIBIT 7.58   CHARTING PEOPLE: SWITCHBOARD HANDLING A PHONE CUSTOMER

Exhibit 7.59 shows a process segment similar to that demonstrated in Exhibit 7.58, but with the call being answered by an answering machine.

The steps along the Customer Via Phone flow line are happening *to* the customer via phone (the customer on the phone). The customer is answered/engaged by the answering system, the customer waits for the order clerk to answer, the customer is answered/engaged by the order clerk, the customer *provides* information to the order clerk, which is used to prepare an order, and the customer is *provided with* an order number.

Note that the process segment in Exhibit 7.59 *does not* capture the response of the customer to the answering machine. This is because the information (i.e., pressing phone buttons or speaking to determine routing) isn't happening *to* the customer, it is happening to the answering system, which is not charted. We could include the answering machine in our chart, as is shown in Exhibit 7.60.

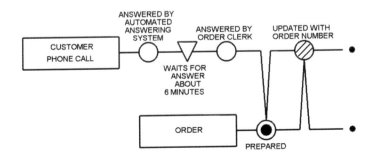

EXHIBIT 7.59   CHARTING PEOPLE: PHONE CUSTOMER IN ANSWERING QUEUE

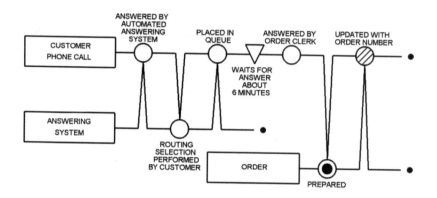

EXHIBIT 7.60 CHARTING PEOPLE: PHONE CUSTOMER AND ANSWERING SYSTEM

Whether you chart the answering machine or not is an issue of detail. The level of detail that you capture in your chart is determined by the objectives of your charting project and is a decision that becomes easier with charting experience.

8

USING PROCESS CHARTS

There is something in the American character that always looks for a better way.

—George W. Bush

The activity involved in preparing process charts provides no value in itself. But when charts are used by employees, they provide value in many ways. Typically, the value of the process charts becomes obvious to the people who use them, and even a one-time-only charting effort becomes a catalyst for additional projects. No greater promotion for process charting exists than first-hand exposure to a successful project. And there is no better way to influence corporate culture toward participative, process-oriented improvement than a handful of quick, visible, successful projects with obvious bottom-line payoffs. Then, if a library of charts becomes available and the activity becomes ongoing, additional benefits become available—beyond improvement.

First, let us look at how charts assist with individual Process Improvement Projects (their original purpose). Then we will cover building the process chart library and the several additional things that the charts can do for us once the library is available. The library has the following purposes:

- To expand from improvement projects into continuous improvement

- To train new hires and employees who are transferred or promoted

- To maintain control:

    o By providing transparency which counters fraud and corruption

    o By meeting regulatory and certification requirements

    o By assisting the audit function

- To establish and maintain a "Mastery Culture"

149

IMPROVING PROCESSES WITH PROJECTS

Real bottom-line value is derived from process charts when they are used to improve the effectiveness and efficiency of the processes. Often the motivation that leads to conducting an improvement project is to correct a problem (e.g., the process has generated costly errors, the process takes too long, the process has failed an audit, the process is not in compliance with new legislation, the process has broken down, and so on).

Unfortunately, the urgency that generates improvement projects encourages shortsighted decisions. Believing that detailed charting will take too long, managers prepare no chart—or, if a chart is prepared, it is so high level that it shows only what most people already know. (Actually, the time required to prepare detailed process charts is generally misunderstood, and usually overestimated. Most processes are easily charted in detail in one or two days' time.) Without the thorough and comprehensive view provided by a detailed process chart, the improvement effort results in changes that correct or lessen the initial problem while often causing undesirable side effects. The more complex the process, the more likely the fix will cause new problems. Where managers are alert to the risk of negative side effects, they sometimes opt to leave the current process untouched and add a totally separate process to address the current problem, further complicating the processes.

Fortunately, the ease with which well-drawn process charts enable people to see what is causing problems and how to correct them makes it is faster to do it right than to cut corners. This can be broken down into four steps:

1. Assemble a team of people who are involved in the process.
2. Prepare a chart of the process as it is now, an "as-is" chart.
3. Walk through the chart with the team. If the project exists to resolve an urgent problem, state the problem in terms of objectives and post the objectives in large print in front of the team as a constant reminder while they work (i.e., to eliminate errors, to reduce cycle time, to fix specific flaws noted in an audit, to comply with new legislation, etc.).
4. Have the team challenge the process step by step.

Sometimes people who are trying to improve get so excited about the first few ideas that surface that they commit to them and close their minds to further opportunities. The following questions provide a pattern that can help them think through the process thoroughly, spotting far more opportunities and arriving at top-quality solutions:

- With each step, first ask, "What are we doing here, and why are we doing it?" If there isn't a good reason, recommend that that step be eliminated. This is the question that produces the most cost-effective changes and should always be asked first. There is no sense in asking the more detailed questions about a work step that should not be done at all. When steps of work are eliminated, there is little or no implementation cost and the benefit equals the full cost of performing that step. Many work steps eliminated by asking this question served a valuable purpose at one time (often years ago), but that purpose has ceased to exist.

- If there is a good reason for performing the step, then ask, "Where is it done and why is it done there?" "When is it done and why is it done at that time?" "Who does it, and why does that person do it?" These questions lead to changes in location, timing, and the person doing the work without changing the task itself, and therefore they are also highly cost effective. Equipment is relocated closer to the people who use it. Schedules are revised to fit with previous and following portions of the process to produce smoother flow. Tasks are shifted to people better able to perform them. Tasks are combined, eliminating the transports and delays between them that occurred as the work flowed between locations and/or people.

- Only after these questions have been asked and answered should the final question be addressed: "How is it done, and why is it done that way?" Although this question can lead to excellent benefits, it also incurs the greatest costs because changing how a task is done generally requires introducing new technology with new equipment, programming, and significant amounts of training. Of course, new technology is important. It is very important, and it should be pursued. But if the organization wants to maximize profits, it will hold off on changing how the steps are performed until after the previous questions have been properly dealt with. (Unfortunately, new technology is so enticing that organizations often leap into it before asking the earlier questions. They miss easy-to-install, high-payoff opportunities, and sometimes wind up having spent a lot of money to automate activities that shouldn't be done at all.)

Using these questions with a process chart provides team members with fresh eyes. They see their work from a new vantage point. They are used to doing the work. They are not used to seeing it as symbols and lines, and as a part of a process. From this new perspective, opportunities for improvement become apparent, and since the people doing the study are thoroughly familiar with the work, their improvements are almost always realistic, practical, and doable.

As team members work their way through the as-is chart, they come up with numerous changes that are easily displayed in a revised chart. When they have done this two or three times, they arrive at a chart that represents the process as they would like it to be—a to-be chart. Now they have two charts, the as-is and the to-be, both drawn step-by-step using precisely the same charting terminology. This paves the way for rigorous handling of approval and implementation activities as follows.

First, team members compare the two charts listing the differences. These differences will become the changes they will recommend in their proposal. Next, they prepare rough but honest estimates of the benefits of each of these changes. They calculate the total benefit, which becomes the opening line of their proposal, followed by the individual changes with the portion of the benefits attributable to each. This usually results in a one-page proposal, which is presented to management for approval.

Only the changes are presented. What is not mentioned will remain as it is. And, because an as-is, to-be model has been used, management has the option of approving the whole of it or any part. (This is not an option if the as-is chart has been skipped and a to-be chart was developed by itself.) Anything not approved remains as it is and the amount of benefit lost is clear. Even if only one recommendation out of ten is approved, there is measurable progress. (Approval rates of 60 to 80 percent are typical, and having all of the recommendations approved is not uncommon.)

Once it has been decided which recommendations are approved for installation, they become the substance for developing a rigorous activity list for implementation. This activity list includes training and whatever changes to programs, written procedures, policies, equipment, forms, and facilities are required for each approved recommendation. These activities are assigned and scheduled. This gives the person coordinating the implementation a clear, manageable picture of what needs to be done.

When the implementation is completed, the to-be chart is reviewed to make sure it is in place as planned. If changes were required that differ from the chart, the chart is revised to reflect the changes and the benefit calculations are adjusted as necessary. Then a final report of benefits is issued and the to-be chart (as revised, if necessary) is relabeled as the new, approved as-is chart and placed in the process chart library.

This is a brief description of how Process Improvement Projects are conducted. Before leaving this subject, it might be helpful to remind the reader of the six different types of projects described earlier in Chapter 3: documentation, improvement, renewal, standardization, development, and maintenance. They differ as follows:

1. *Documentation projects* involve only an as-is chart. There is no attempt to improve. There are apt to be many of these projects during the early stages of building a process-chart library.

2. *Improvement projects* and *renewal projects* both involve an as-is chart and a to-be chart. The difference is the extent of the study. On an improvement project, the team looks for the changes that can be installed with the least disruption to the organization, generally avoiding major restructuring of departments and totally new systems. With renewal projects, there are no holds barred.

3. *Standardization projects* involve two or more as-is charts and usually one to-be chart. They are especially helpful following a merger.

4. *Development projects* involve only a to-be chart because the process does not yet exist. In development projects, the detailed charting method enables the charter to think through the new process much as an architect thinks through a new building. For the architect, it is important to work out the problems on paper before concrete is poured. For the process designer, it is equally beneficial to work out the problems on paper before people are hired or transferred and assigned to tasks that have not been thought through.

5. *Maintenance projects* are the backbone of the process-chart library and continuous improvement. They are usually the quickest and easiest projects, and they are described in detail under continuous improvement, later in this chapter.

BUILDING A PROCESS LIBRARY

Imagine having a library of process charts that provides a clear picture of all of the work that occurs in your organization. Put that thought in mind and get started. A simple folder structure is sufficient to start. When the first process is charted, store it where it can be readily accessed but not modified without approval. When changes are approved and implemented, a new chart is placed in the chart library as the approved as-is chart. The library manager transfers the old as-is chart to an archive folder, replacing it with the new one in the approved folder. This is a simple view of process-library management, but it doesn't have to be much more difficult than this.

Before long, a significant portion of the organization is properly documented in the chart library. And—its costs are covered! It is a byproduct of an improvement effort. The benefits produced by improvement far exceed the cost of building the library. Compare this with very expensive efforts at documentation where the principal purpose is the documentation itself.

To assure that the library continues to provide benefits to the organization, there needs to be a person responsible for maintaining it. This person should be good at charting. At the outset, this person will spend a lot of time preparing charts and facilitating projects. As the library grows, more time is spent maintaining the library, sustaining the continuous improvement effort, and making current approved charts available to new employees, to employees who have been promoted or transferred, to auditors, and to anyone else who wants to know how the processes of the organization work.

It is important that the people throughout the organization know about the library and know how to use it, and the person managing the library makes this happen. The quality of process understanding throughout the organization will then grow out of fog and into confident mastery, and the person managing the library will gradually accumulate a massive understanding of how the organization works.

A well-managed, process-chart library takes improvement from the project level to the organizational culture level. It provides a fundamental structure for continuous improvement, a remarkable training source, the documentation required for regulatory requirements and certification requirements, and a powerful boost to the audit function. It frees the organization of a great deal of bureaucratic fog by giving the employees and managers a clear picture of how their processes work. And it bears a negative cost (i.e., building it generates benefits that exceed its cost). First, let us look at continuous improvement.

CONTINUOUS IMPROVEMENT

Many organizations have committed to continuous improvement, but they have failed to give it a self-sustaining structure. As long as the effort lacks a self-sustaining structure, it must be constantly promoted or it will fade. It doesn't take much distraction to interrupt the promotion. The key to keeping it going is the process-chart library.

Any major event such as a merger, reorganization, the loss of key personnel, a bad sales year, critical legislative changes, and so on can quickly undercut the continuous improvement effort if it lacks structure. The irony is that all of these situations can be dealt with far more effectively with the help of continuous improvement. But, continuous improvement becomes unmanageable during crisis if it has not been institutionalized. And the distraction does not need to be a major event to cause it to wane and disappear. The process-chart library institutionalizes continuous improvement. When a major event shakes the organization, the appropriate process charts are at hand to assist in responding to the event. Continuous improvement, rather than appearing expendable during crisis, appears indispensable. The charts were there when we needed them.

Here is how the process-chart library is used to give continuous improvement an ongoing structure. As the charts accumulate in the library, they carry last-approval dates. At a preset interval, say once a year, or at an earlier time if requested by the process owner, the library manager prints a copy of the chart and sends it to its work area for review. The receipt of the chart triggers the formation of a team of employees to go through it to see if it still matches the way the process is being performed and to question whether the process is working satisfactorily. If the chart is still correct as is and it is working well, it is simply reapproved and returned to the library manager, who updates the history on that chart with a fresh approval date. If the team finds that changes have occurred in the way the work is processed, they mark up the chart and return it. The library manager revises the chart, checking the revisions at the work area, and then places the new, approved chart in the library. If the review team decides that the process is now ripe for improvement, they initiate an improvement project. (This will generally be the case when the process owner has requested the review.) The chart that they are reviewing becomes the as-is chart, which provides a baseline for an improvement project. The project then produces a new, improved approved chart, which updates the library. These activities simultaneously maintain the chart library and the continuous improvement effort.

Trying to manage a complex organization without a chart library is like trying to build a complex machine or a large building without prints. Most organizations that build complex machines or large buildings have long ago learned how indispensable the prints were, and they have institutionalized the work of providing them. Unfortunately, most organizations have not arrived at the same indispensable view of process charts. As a result, they do a lot of muddling through which they blame on bureaucracy and accept as inevitable. The alternative to bureaucracy is for organizations to master their processes. We will come back to this subject at the end of this chapter.

TRAINING

Whenever a new hire comes on board or whenever someone is promoted or reassigned to new work, a notice is sent to the library. The library manager prepares a set of charts for the processes that these people will be working on and delivers them to the person who is in the new position. These charts provide overviews that show the employees just how their tasks fit into the entire process. They see what happens to the work before they get it and what happens after they are finished with it. This shows them their part in the bigger picture, a vital ingredient for figuring out how to handle unusual transactions without causing undue difficulty in other parts of the process. It speeds the learning process that takes them from simply following directions to being the masters of their work.

This learning is commonly referred to as *knowing the ropes*. With the muddling-through model mentioned earlier, learning the ropes can take many years; in some cases, it simply doesn't happen. Employees continue throughout their careers performing tasks (that often appear to be mindless tasks) exactly as they have been instructed. They lack the understanding needed whenever they have to process something that is a little bit different. With process charts, the ropes are spelled out and available from the start.

In addition to helping to train the people who do the work, the chart library provides a powerful aid to new supervisors and managers. It provides them with a clear picture of what their employees do and how that work fits into other parts of the organization. When people are promoted or hired to fill supervisory or management positions, they cannot hope to know the details of what they are responsible for. They can talk to their people and learn a lot, and they should do that. But this will not give them a comprehensive understanding of the tasks in their department and will provide little knowledge of how those tasks fit into other parts of the organization.

Do not confuse this learning of the processes with matching the skills of the employees who do the work. Supervisors and managers do not need to know and should not get involved in all the details of their employees' work. The process chart provides a picture of how tasks fit together. It gives them the bigger picture. It does not show the skills to perform their tasks.

Skills come from training and with experience. For instance, when a doctor makes an entry on a patient's chart, the skill to make a proper entry is the result of years of education and experience. When an underwriter enters a code on an insurance application, the skill that results in a proper entry likely came from several years of study to pass certification tests. In each case, the process chart simply shows a single symbol, an Add/Alter symbol, with a few words such as "diagnosis and prescription entered" or "risk code entered." It is obvious that those few words do not begin to describe the skills of doing the tasks.

The two examples just cited both involve professional tasks. A similar relationship holds for nonprofessionals such as clerks working on loading docks, accounting clerks, cashiers, file clerks, and so on. While the extent of their preparation varies, employees who want to develop skill will find the opportunity to do it on any task, and the skill they develop will not show up on the process chart.

The training value of the charts is different for employees doing the work and for supervisors and managers overseeing it. For employees who perform the tasks, the chart shows very little of what they need to know to be able to do those tasks skillfully but provides valuable understanding of how those tasks fit into the big picture. For supervisors and managers, the chart shows much of what they need to know (sometimes all they need to know) about the tasks that they supervise, but it also shows the big picture, which is their responsibility. Managing processes, keeping the work flowing, is an important part of the responsibility of supervisors and managers.

(*Note:* When high-level charts are used, they do not show the steps that the employees perform. Therefore, they provide little training value to either the employees doing the work or to their supervisors and managers. Employees who do the work are not able to find their work and its connection with the big picture, and the supervisors and managers do not see the steps of the work that accomplish the big picture.)

Study of the processes with which they are involved is an important part of the training of all employees as they start in on a new job. Charts supplied by a chart library accomplish this quickly and comprehensively. It sometimes comes as a surprise (because the charts look unfamiliar and a bit intimidating) that they are quite easy to learn. Charts that contain 100 or more symbols are not difficult to memorize. This is because the symbols appear in the sequence in which they are performed, and the lines clearly show the flow. If 100 or more symbols were placed on a piece of paper as unrelated tasks, they would be very hard to learn. The mind would have to organize them logically to remember them. The structure of the chart does this for us.

Finally, the charts aid training because of what they are. They provide a focus on process. There is a natural tendency in all organizations toward increasing complexity. The more complex the organization becomes, the more pronounced this tendency will be. Complexity breeds more complexity. Where there is insufficient focus on processes, processes grow beyond the understanding of the people. The people become locked into them. They are not the masters of their processes. A keen focus on process, accompanied by detailed charts that effectively portray them, puts the people in charge of, with mastery over, their processes.

In addition to providing charts to employees for training, the library can also provide segments of these charts printed out in narrative, Playscript[1] format, as shown in Exhibit 8.1. This format converts a chart segment into a list of steps with a numbered outline structure. When the segment being charted gets to an alternative, the numbering shifts to subnumbering.

Fork Lift Operator	**1**		Starts at loading dock - Delivers Shipping Papers to receiving office and places them in the inbox.
Receiving Clerk	**2**		Checks to see if receipt is for office supplies, janitorial supplies, or lab supplies.
	3a		If the receipt is for office supplies or janitorial supplies, sends an e-mail notice to the office manager.
	3b		If the receipt is for lab supplies:
		1	Check to see if the receipt is in the Order System.
		2a	If the receipt is in the Order System, GOTO Step 4.
		2b	If the receipt is a new order:
		1	Completes a 595 online form and prints it.
		2	Carries the printed copy of the 595 to the Lab and gives it to the Lab Assistant.

EXHIBIT 8.1 SEGMENT OF A PROCESS CHART PRINTED IN PLAYSCRIPT FORMAT

Playscript format is limited to fairly small sequences of steps and therefore lacks the structure to display the interconnectedness of a process. However, it does a good job of showing portions of a process in narrative form. It maintains sequence well and has an advantage in that several steps performed by the same person can be combined under a single step number. This has been done in Step 1 in the example shown in Exhibit 8.1. The work of the lift truck operator would appear as two steps on the process chart, a transportation symbol to show the delivery of the shipping papers, and a handling operation to show placing the shipping papers in the inbox.

Before leaving the discussion of the use of the process-chart library for training, it is appropriate to include a few words about personnel turnover and vulnerability. Some training-related situations beg to be charted. These include strategic processes that are fully or primarily handled by only one person and processes associated with high turnover. Left undocumented, one-person processes and high-turnover processes put the organization in a precarious and perhaps even irresponsible position. Documenting these processes greatly reduces this vulnerability.

LIBRARY AND CONTROL

How organizations manage their processes speaks volumes about their integrity. In some organizations, secrecy, manipulation, and distrust dominate. Obscured by complex bureaucratic rules, customers and vendors are cheated, employees are downsized, and bank accounts are milked. Corporate clutter and the speed at which operations roll on assure that little will surface until comfortably after the fact. When well-intentioned efforts to correct these problems create rules that add more layers of bureaucracy, the edge goes to those who learn the rules and decide to get around them without being seen.

All sorts of organizations suffer. They don't have to be profit making. The main mission of any organization can become secondary to private agendas when operations lie hidden behind a bureaucratic fog. Quality deteriorates in health care, in courts of law, in schools, in government—in fact, wherever convoluted processes obscure the work and invite irresponsible behavior.

TRANSPARENCY

The process-chart library can play an important role in maintaining organizational integrity. The key is transparency. Documenting the processes and subjecting them to review by knowledgeable employees at regular intervals provides transparency. Generally speaking, the more open the operations of an organization, the more fair play we can expect. The less visible the operations of an organization, the more opportunity there is for unfairness and the more people will suspect that it is there. When organizations support open, wholesome behavior, they strengthen feelings of trust. If they do enough of it, people can relax and focus on doing their best. Open, wholesome behavior also encourages more of the same behavior, building a climate of trust.

REGULATORY REQUIREMENTS SUCH AS SARBANES-OXLEY

The Sarbanes–Oxley Act was a response to public outcry over fraudulent corporate behavior. One of the key features of this legislation is the requirement that corporations document their processes. Many companies reacted to this requirement by complaining about the costs they would incur. But if they go about it properly, building a library of detailed process charts, the effort should generate benefits well in excess of the costs.

Of course, there are many ways that processes can be documented. If high-level charts are used, the requirement may be superficially satisfied. If the processes are documented in narrative form rather than with charts, the effort will be far more costly. And, while both of these efforts may satisfy the requirement, neither will provide the rich benefits of a detailed process-chart library. It would be a shame not to turn the requirement to an advantage and have it pay for itself.

CERTIFICATION SUCH AS ISO

The same holds true for the requirements of ISO certification. The rules of ISO certification are open regarding how work processes are documented. Essentially, certification requires that an organization "says what it does and does what it says." Processes must be documented, and periodic examination must show that the documentation is being followed.

One of the drawbacks that companies have experienced with ISO certification is that after spending a considerable amount of money and effort preparing their documentation, they find it difficult and costly to update it. Unless documentation is easy to update, it quickly becomes outdated. As changes creep into operations, the organization falls out of compliance. Or, an organization can set a moratorium on change in order to maintain compliance, stifling workers by forcing them to follow procedures that grow increasingly out of date. ISO certification made this dilemma painfully clear. Documentation that is difficult to revise becomes like an organizational straightjacket, preventing improvement. This will apply just the same to documentation prepared to satisfy the requirements of Sarbanes–Oxley or any other regulation.

The key to avoiding this documentation disadvantage is to maintain the documentation in an easily updatable format. A detailed process chart library meets this need very well. As the library is being used to institutionalize continuous improvement, it simultaneously assures that the charts are kept current with operations. And it generates major benefits while doing so.

HELPING THE AUDIT

When the work processes are audited, the person responsible for the process library can quickly and easily provide the auditors with charts from which they can get a detailed understanding of the processes they are reviewing. As they read the charts, they find that most of the questions that they normally need to ask in order to become familiar with a process are answered. The charts identify each document with a label, followed by symbols that clearly show every time information is entered or altered, where the inspections occur, who sees the documents, and where they are filed.

It is imperative that a process library be developed and maintained if we are to become masters of our processes. Employees need to know what is in the library and how to get to it. Involving the auditors with the library is one more way of building it into the culture of the organization.

ESTABLISHING A CULTURE OF MASTERY

When people work with detailed process charts, they gain improved understandings of how those processes work. They also gain better understandings of how their work fits in with the work of others in different areas of the organization. The more they work with the process charts, the clearer things become. As this type of activity becomes a part of the organizational culture, the bureaucratic fog thins and lifts.

These understandings increase confidence. Employees become more confident in themselves and they become more confident in the organization. They can see that the organization's processes are well-defined, understood, and under control. Where the employees also see portions of those processes that were developed on improvement projects in which they participated, they sense pride.

This is healthy activity. It facilitates openness, cooperation, creativity, and mature responsible behavior. It does this, not by badgering or preaching, but by creating situations that call for these behaviors. These situations call for the behaviors of masters.

MASTERY

Masters are people who dig into the realities of their work and develop detailed understandings that permit them to perform with excellence. Many employees go through their careers with little taste of mastery—some because they never have the opportunity, others because they choose to avoid it. Many get caught up in childish games, posturing, looking busy, beating the system, and thinking they are getting away with it. Then there are those, who may have been quite the masters a while back, who have become tired and bored, and who use their ingenuity to snuggle down into the bureaucratic fog and rest.

The activity of reviewing a detailed process chart is an exercise in mastery. Regardless of what behaviors people may have gotten into the habit of, when they are put to this task, they are being called upon to act like masters. When this happens with a team of people, they tend to reinforce each other in the direction of mastery. With a good facilitator, this happens quickly and powerfully. It reaches into the team members and brings out enthusiasm for the task. Then, when they see the results of their efforts incorporated into their work, their enthusiasm is rewarded with pride.

The process-chart library is the structural key to building masterful process-improvement behavior into the organizational culture. But it won't happen if the people of the organization ignore the library. It won't happen if the library is sparsely stocked. (It doesn't require that 100 percent of the processes of the organization be charted, but the closer the better.) It won't happen if the leadership of the organization doesn't support it.

A serious charting effort to build the library is necessary. The person managing the library must distribute charts to all employees on new jobs and to the proper work areas for scheduled review. And senior managers must insist that the reviews be given serious attention. When these things happen, the people of the organization become better people and the organization approaches becoming as good as its people.

ENDNOTE

1. Leslie H. Matthies, *The Playscript Procedure: A New Tool of Administration* (Office Publications, 1961).

9

PROCESS CHART STORIES

The productivity of people requires...above all...the willingness to ask employees systematically and to listen to their answers. It requires acceptance of the fact that the person who does the job is likely to know more about it than the person who supervises...

—Peter F. Drucker

Detail process charting experts are scattered among organizations around the world. They are on the loading docks, in the data entry departments, and in the accounting departments. They are analysts, engineers, clerks, and supervisors. They are customer service representatives and managers. They are people who have decided that they want to understand their processes better, and they have taken the time to learn a technique that truly allows them to understand their business processes. They are consultants who have decided that if they can understand their clients' processes better, they can serve them better.

The following testimonials are provided by a handful of these experts. They cite the real value of detailed process charts for improvement, for training, for transparency, for ISO certification, to satisfy regulatory requirements, and for their contributing effect on corporate culture.

(*Note:* Because these are all people with whom the Ben Graham Corporation has worked directly, their comments frequently refer to Graham charting, Graham Charting Software, and the Graham methodology. Graham charts and the Graham improvement methodology were first developed in the 1940s by the author's grandfather, Ben S. Graham. After his death in 1960, the work was continued and considerably expanded by the author's father, Ben S. Graham Jr. In 1990, Ben S. Graham Jr. converted the charting from pencil drawings using plastic templates to the Graham Charting Software, which all of these people have used. During these 50-plus years, three generations of Ben Grahams have worked with many thousands of people, representing more than a thousand organizations. These stories provide a taste of what has happened with a few of those people.)

ALLEN BACK

PROCESS IMPROVEMENT CONSULTANT

Allen has completed a number of projects that have generated large savings. He has seen a very effective blend of detailed process charting with Six Sigma.

I have worked in consulting more than five years. During that time, I have practiced the sound process-improvement methods taught by Ben S. Graham. In recent years, I have studied and practiced the Six Sigma methodology. While attending the Six Sigma Black Belt course, I was disappointed in the cursory emphasis given to process improvement, since process focus is the heart of improving business performance. The basic charting methods suggested in the Six Sigma course are effective when looking at a process in a macro view. However, the Graham charts provide more of the detail needed when analyzing a process. I recently facilitated a project in the health industry that resulted in more than $200,000 in savings. We charted the process using both the basic Six Sigma method and a Graham chart. The team found the Graham chart easier to follow and much more effective in presenting the relative facts needed to recommend improvements.

MERLE LAIRD

BUSINESS ANALYST AND PRINCIPAL OF
SYSTEMS CADENCE (CONSULTING)

Merle began using detailed process charts back when the effort was called work simplification, and she refers to her detailed process charts as work simplification charts. She has more recently used these charts for ISO documentation, for new business development, for manufacturing processes, and for regulatory compliance.

Near the beginning of my career as a business analyst, I simply charted (all done by hand, I may add) for the sole purpose of documenting the information flow and what forms a business or organization was using. These charts were used to simplify work procedures and reduce the number of documents within a process. A new chart would be drawn up (again, by hand using a template) and used in a presentation format for staff participation and training. This presentation would demonstrate the changes that were made and what the employees' new responsibilities within the process were.

As my business grew, so did the areas in which I used work simplification (WS) flowcharts within my business. I started to use WS flowcharts to collect and document processes for ISO registration, referencing form numbers and safety standards right along with the procedures. These were very useful in training the staff in ISO requirements and allowing them to understand the interconnection between departments and how what they did affected so many other areas of the business. By this time, the WS flowcharting was all computerized and it was very easy to update and adjust the charts when improvements were required to get a company ready for ISO. Procedures were often written directly from the flowcharts and done with ease, ensuring that steps were not left out. This made the standard operating procedures easy for the employees to follow since it was all "their" work steps and "their" documentation. Again, training was made easy for the employees and management alike.

A new manufacturing company was being created, and products were being designed and built. Systems Cadence was contracted to flowchart the steps of manufacturing, charting each part (including part number, bin number, and quantity) and any subassemblies that were required for the finished product. The flowcharts referenced all engineering drawings, part lists, subassemblies, safety standards, decals, name plates, forms, and associated procedures. Once the product was assembled, quality inspected, and packaged...the flowchart described the shipping process. The company was able to get the production line up and going very quickly and later was able to adjust easily to manage growing pains. Written procedures were developed based on these production flowcharts....Training for new staff was very efficient and effective since the flow of parts was documented in a visual format instead of just written.

A few years ago, the Canadian government developed legislation to help protect personal information within public and private organizations, including nonprofit. Personal Information Protection and Electronic Documents Act (PIPEDA) is the act, and in short, it requires all organizations that have personal information to develop policies and procedures that state their privacy statement, privacy policies and procedures, how they handle third-party transfer of information, and how the company deals with access to information and the complaint process from either an employee or client. Flowcharting has been a very powerful auditing tool for our company as I interview the staff and management as to the information that the company/organization has—where and how it is stored, whether it is computer or paper, and who has access to it. Flowcharting is just a natural way to first obtain the information from the employees and then to complete the audit based on the information received. The flowcharts are then used to evaluate the security required under the new legislation and ultimately used to train all employees. Policies and procedures are developed from these flowcharts to ensure that everyone is singing from the same song sheet.

These are just three situations where flowcharting has been so valuable within my business...and let's not forget the absolutely ultimate use of gathering information from employees: using it for process improvement and quality assurance. Isn't that what got the business world using work simplification flowcharting in the first place—whether it is manually performed or computer generated?

BILL ROACH

CRM, EDMS COORDINATOR, STATE OF NORTH DAKOTA, ITD/RECORDS MANAGEMENT

Bill is involved in an exciting effort within the state government in North Dakota. They have built a large library with hundreds of process charts.

Detailed process charts are the key to understanding and communicating business processes. The State of North Dakota uses Graham Business Processing Charts to document existing business processes, including any exceptions or deviations. The original chart is analyzed to improve efficiency and apply technology. Staff who work with the process, as well as those involved with inputs and outputs, actively participate in the entire effort. Once completed, the new chart is used to train staff, generate procedures, program workflows, and modify business applications. Very often we find that the charting effort was the first time all of the participants sat down to discuss in detail what they do and its impact. The interaction of the charting process often unleashes individual creativity and creates a sense of ownership and accomplishment. It has been my experience that the effort changes many from being passive bystanders to active participants in the workplace.

Detailed process charts are the key to understanding and communicating business processes. High-level views may be acceptable for executive presentations, but they are worthless for the folks in the trenches. The best comparison I can think of is to compare business process charts to maps. A globe will suffice if all you want to do is show someone where you are going. But if you really want to get there, you need a detailed map, complete with expanded views of congested areas, alternate routes, and travel options. With only a globe as a guide, you have little chance of reaching your destination.

HECTOR PIÑA

PRESIDENT, AKADEMOS, CONSULTANT, LATIN AMERICA

Hector works throughout Latin America. Here he tells about an outstanding experience in Sao Paulo.

One of the most rewarding experiences that I recall from my professional life is my involvement with the work simplification methodology. It is amazing to observe how a few symbols and conventions, with enthusiastic participation, management support, and an adequate facilitating process, might change the spirit of the people in charge of the job, the rework might be reduced, and the overall productivity might be increased.

One example is the work performed in the Brazilian subsidiary of a worldwide delivery packaging company. The Brazilian headquarters were located in Sao Paulo, Brazil. From that city, they received and dispatched packages within Brazil and between Brazil and the rest of the world. Two major airports, two hours by car from each other, were used by this company as its hub in order to receive, nationalize, distribute, and coordinate the delivery of the different packages. A complex network of ground and air transportation followed the arrival of packages in order to ensure the final delivery to the destination.

The problem for which this company requested help had to do with assurance of the delivery time of the packages, as well as the entire administrative process for collecting payment from key customers. Key customers, relatively few in number but high on invoicing, were complaining of tardiness in the delivery services. However, the key problem was on the delivering-invoicing-collecting process that was affecting cash flow. It was a time-related issue that needed to be solved immediately.

A team composed of highly motivated and experienced employees was created. Management allowed time to collect, chart, and analyze the information. The project was announced and a period of three weeks was allowed for the team to present results and recommendations for change. The process was charted from the reception of packages up to the generation of the invoices to the clients. Data were compiled from within the records and validated from an interdisciplinary perspective. Proposed solutions were analyzed and quantified. The solutions were also validated with relevant providers that had a direct involvement in the overall process, such as banking institutions that were responsible for receiving payments from the clients once the invoice was sent. Creativity, a sense of reality, and facts, altogether, played a key part of the improvement process. Needless to say, it required hard work in order to understand a very complex process and to summarize it on a lengthy but understandable chart. However, pride and cheerfulness were also a part of the team; finally ideas and efforts were in hand to provide a tangible and practical solution to a complex problem.

At the end of the agreed period, a presentation was delivered by the members of the team to the top executives of the company. Mixed feelings of surprise, disbelief, and positive expectations were shared by all meeting participants. These feelings arose simply from the proposed changes and expected results: drastic reductions in time for invoicing (almost three weeks) and an increase of several hundred thousands of U.S. dollars, monthly, in the company's cash flow just by reducing the invoicing time process. The same changes also improved the quality of the service of delivering packages. All the proposed solutions were practical, cost-efficient, and, in some cases, only required management approval to be implemented.

SHARON CUNNINGHAM

CONSULTANT AND SIX SIGMA BLACK BELT

Sharon has provided several examples including one where detailed charts provided the transparency to discover a fraud. In others, she used charts to set up new procedures for reengineering, for training, for ISO certification, and for Six Sigma projects.

On one project, we identified six types of errors in the process for producing a product that was delivered to a customer. The process included multiple computer systems on different operating platforms. Many of the problems occurred at the interface points between the systems. The existing process for reconciliation was very onerous, sometimes taking three days to identify the affected customer. The project reduced the cycle time for reconciliation by 85 percent and improved both customer and employee satisfaction. A surprising result of this project was that one of the six sources of errors turned out to be a disgruntled employee falsifying company documents that identified the customer who was affected by the error in the process. The employee would work for a few hours of what could be (perhaps) three days that it would take to identify the correct customer, and, if not successful, would randomly select a customer and create the required paperwork. The detailed process charting and subsequent analysis of errors pointed out the employee's activities. The employee was subsequently fired, and personnel used some of the documentation discovered in the analysis phase of this project during the personnel action.

We developed more than 20 new processes for a start-up insurance division, ensuring appropriate system design and superior system controls. The detailed process charts and procedures provided the documentation used for education of new employees. The new division started up with no problems with any of the processes thus defined.

We reengineered the process for producing renewals on credit cards. We reduced the cycle time by 50 percent and reduced the number of forms required from 13 to 1. The project and the detailed charting methodology were well received by the employees. To train them on the new process, flows were printed 4 feet high and about 40 feet long. (Large scale was used to be legible from several feet away.) The chart wrapped most of the way around a large conference room. We walked the employees around the room, reading the flow charts to teach them the new process. The ability to print charts in this way is a very useful feature of the Graham Charting Software.

We reengineered the process for the reconciliation of postage for customer statements. We reduced the cycle time from over 30 days to less than 48 hours. This greatly improved the controls over a significant amount of money.

We reengineered a process for a new software library management application. We identified 12 potential problems in the design phase. The earlier a problem is identified in the development cycle, the less money it takes to correct the problem. This project was such a success that management required that this methodology be used in other software development applications.

We utilized the Graham detailed process charting methodology to develop all of the process charts for a medium-sized company seeking ISO 9000 certification. ISO requires a company to "*say what you do, and do what you say.*" The detailed Graham process charts serve three purposes: (1) documentation of the process; (2) training material for new employees; and (3) providing audit guides for the self-audit required in the ISO process.

We utilized the Graham detailed process charting as a key tool in several Six Sigma projects. Process mapping is a key requirement in the Six Sigma methodology. Everything else is built from an understanding of the customer wants and the actual process currently occurring. Another use of process charting in the Six Sigma methodology is in the development of the "after" process chart, showing the new and improved process. The detailed process charting available in the Graham tool is ideal for identifying the control points in the process that guarantee the improvements will stay in place.

TODD RIGBY

PROCESS IMPROVEMENT MANAGER, WHEELER MACHINERY CO.

Todd has facilitated a number of projects that have generated significant benefits. He has also seen these efforts produce very positive effects on his company's culture.

Detail process charts are the principal tool in the Process Improvement Program at Wheeler Machinery Co. The program has enabled Wheeler to accomplish what is often thought of as mutually exclusive goals—driving cost out of operations and preserving corporate knowledge. The organization consistently saves $100,000 to $250,000 per project, per year, without the loss of a single job.

Employees, with the knowledge and experience they possess, are Wheeler's single greatest asset. Detail process charts help us tap into that experience. Too often, companies looking for short-term cost reductions make the mistake of reducing their work force. While they may have lower operating costs in the short term, their long-term costs increase and their competitiveness decreases since they no longer can work as efficiently as they did before they lost a portion of their corporate knowledge base. That is coupled with the fact they are still burdened with inefficient processes.

Process improvement has almost single-handedly changed the company culture from apathy to high performance. Employees have learned that change is good. Through process improvement, they have removed inefficiencies from their jobs, and their satisfaction and motivation have increased tremendously. These employees now feel empowered to work hard at making everything they do better because they realize that the company cares about them and wants them to be efficient and productive.

Often, the only way to find inefficiencies such as redundancy, poor order of operation, or lack of controls is through diagramming the process utilizing Graham process charts. This simple but elegant tool allows even an untrained individual to quickly identify process gaps, overlaps, and redundancies. It is also an excellent platform for redesigning processes where controls can be placed properly, efficiency can be optimized, and people can accomplish more accurate work in less time.

VALERIE RAUSCH

BUSINESS ANALYST, FINNING (CANADA)

Valerie comments on the ease with which employee teams take on the ownership of improvement projects once they have seen the charts.

My favorite part of the Graham methodology is the walk-through of an as-is chart for the first time with a project team. It never fails to amaze me how quickly team members begin to take ownership of their process and become excited about the prospect of change. They are surprised by the level of detail I am able to capture using the Ben Graham charting process. Each and every time I see the same reaction: "Wow, is this what we do?" Once that transfer of ownership takes place, getting the group to improve their process is easy; they do most of the work on their own.

During a recent review of the service repair process at one of our medium-sized branches, the chart revealed that significant time was being spent at the end of the process looking up job codes and component code descriptions due to insufficient information being provided on the customer proposal. This was delaying the process significantly. Changes were made to the process that ensured all required information was provided on the proposal before a work order was opened. Better planning up front dramatically reduced the billing effort at the back end. Even though steps were added to the front end of the process, the net result was more than 50 work steps eliminated.

BEN S. GRAHAM JR.

CHAIRMAN, THE BEN GRAHAM CORPORATION

Ben has been involved with projects for over forty years and here describes a few memorable ones.

During the 1970s, I helped on a project at the Bureau of Drugs in Rockville, Maryland. We prepared about a dozen charts and then reviewed them with about 35 employees including medical doctors, pharmacologists, statisticians, and various administrative personnel. The changes they came up with resulted in doubling the productivity of the Bureau, measured in drug reviews processed. There were savings calculated at over a million dollars, and they cut review time down to the point that they were completing almost all of their reviews within the legally prescribed time limits, something they had found very difficult to do before. The project was completed up to implementation in 15 weeks. Implementation, which included major facilities changes (ripping out walls and rebuilding offices) as well as changing all of the forms, was completed over the next nine months (one and one-half months per division). Much of the success of this project I credit to the outstanding support of the director of the Bureau, Dr. Richard Crout, and the tenacity of the project leader,

Jerry Deighton. There were a number of awards granted to people as a result of this project, including myself.

More recently, in 1998 I was asked by then city manager of Dayton, Ohio, Valerie Lemmie, to sit in on a Development Task Force. Business was leaving the city center, and there had been no major new building there for decades. The task force was made up of key players in the city who wanted to see this turned around. I joined the task force and soon found out that this was the third such task force formed. The others had met quite a few years previously, completed their deliberations, made their reports—and nothing had happened. I also learned that a number of the people on this task force had previously served on one or both of the previous two. At the end of the second meeting, I talked to Dusty Hall, assistant city manager, who was sitting in on the meetings. I told him that I knew very little of what the task force was discussing and really didn't care what they came up with, but if they would let me chart the building permits process and work with the people who did that processing, I would see that whatever they came up with would happen. This was cleared. We charted the process in one day, approximately 400 steps. At the next meeting of the task force, the charts were hanging on the wall. The people on the task force arrived in the room, gravitated over to the charts, and started reading them. They were impressed by the detail and the professional appearance of the charts, and then something special happened. The spirit in the room changed. There was a general feeling that they were going to do it this time. The task force came up with eight major recommendations. Then an improvement team was formed, representing the different areas of building permit processing: building, zoning, engineering, fire, water, structural, housing, and plumbing/heating/electrical. The team members studied the charts and worked out how to accomplish each of the eight recommendations. Within a year, the building-permits people of the city moved into a one-stop shop, and since that time the city has seen the building of a minor league ballpark, a new office building, a new performing arts center, and a major park area along the Miami River, which runs through town. This project had excellent top management support from the city manager, and from John Thomas, who managed the new one-stop shop.

A while back, I trained a young man by the name of Richard Johnston, who was working for EG&G Idaho. We talked in the evening about some of the things he might do. Shortly after the training, I got a somewhat nervous call from Richard. He told me that he had gotten into a discussion about work simplification during lunch with the company president, who seemed to become quite interested. So Richard decided to take a chance. He told the president, "If you will get me $50,000 to start a work simplification program, I'll get you $5 million back within a year". The president turned to one of the men who was with him and told him to set up an account of $50,000 to start a work simplification program. Shortly thereafter, we put 50 people through work simplification training. At the end of the training, each person trained was asked to select a small project in their work area, chart it, form a team of four or five people and go over the chart with them, see what ideas they could come up with, rechart the process, and have this done in 12 days. Then they would bring their charts to another training session where we would show them how to calculate the benefits. At the end of the 12 days, 35 of the 50 people had completed to-be charts. We calculated $680,000 worth of benefits, of which $60,000 was already installed. The program grew, much of it due to the enthusiastic and effective efforts of Richard. At the end of the year, he was able to report $35 million in installed savings.

Perhaps my favorite story, this one dates back to the 1950s. In 1959, my father trained a young man by the name of Hector Riquezes, who was working for Creole Petroleum (the largest oil firm in Venezuela). Hector charted a shipping process at the Caripito Terminal, and when the team reviewed it, they found that no one was using any of the information. The people who were doing the processing all knew what they were doing and how to do it, and the information they were processing was being dutifully filed. They had files going back many years. But no one was using any of it. At this point, Hector did what I recommend anyone should do under those circumstances. He dug into it to find out why the process was set up in the first place. (If you don't know what a thing is for, it is a little risky to get rid of it. But if you know what it used to be for and that reason no longer exists, you can confidently get rid of it.) Hector found out that the reason they were processing this data was to supply information to schedule oil ships to rendezvous off of the island of Trinidad and form up into convoys to sail to Europe during World War II. Of course, this was 1959 and WWII had ended in 1945. Not bad, eh? Only 14 years. What do you think those people would have been doing with those records in 1960 if Hector had not done his project in 1959? How about 1961? When would it have ended? I have a fantasy that along about 1979 or 1980, when much of the world was caught up in the idea of the paperless office, they would have automated it. Back then, a lot of thinking ran along the lines that if you automate something, it is bound to be better, so there is no need to get into questions like, "Why are we doing this at all?" So today they would have an automated process for scheduling phantom convoys that hadn't sailed for over half a century. This project gave an excellent boost to the early part of Hector's career, and through the years he did well. When I worked with him in 1983, he was a Director of Lagoven, the new name of Creole. A few years later, he was a Director of Petróleos de Venezuela, S.A. (PDVSA), the holding company that controls the oil industry of Venezuela. Throughout his career he was a strong supporter of work simplification. Near the end of his career, the president of Venezuela pulled him out of PDVSA to head up industrial training for the country. A fine man and a fine career.

10

SUMMARY

Drive thy business or it will drive thee.

—Benjamin Franklin

Process charts have been used for the best part of the past century to help people understand their work better. However, there is little literature available that carefully describes how to prepare detailed process charts. Descriptions of the methodology described in this book are difficult to find. Nevertheless, documents published by university professors, professional organizations, the federal government, and companies like IBM, RCA, Ford Motor Company, Procter & Gamble, and Standard Register have attested to its value.

This book attempts to arm the reader with enough knowledge of the work simplification approach to process charting to enable them to prepare good detailed process charts. This skill can be developed by most people who are comfortable working with diagrams and disciplined enough to adhere to a rigorous methodology. This chapter is a review of some of the principal considerations for successful process charting and may serve as a quick reminder to people who are developing their charting and their improvement-project facilitation skills.

DEFINE A PROJECT

Select a Process to Study

- Any activity can be improved.
- Problems are *not* a prerequisite for improvement.

Identify problems begging for improvement:

- Customers (clients, constituents, etc.) are dissatisfied with performance.
- It takes too long to process an order.
- The defect rate is too high.

173

- The backlog is too large.
- There is too much confusion.
- The system must conform to new regulations.
- The process seems too complicated.

Get Appropriate Approvals/Buy-in to Conduct a Project

The executive (process owner) of the project must sign off on the project. The process owner's span of control includes all the areas being studied. Therefore, the process owner must do the following:

- Approve the project
- Establish project objectives
- Outline the project scope
- Visibly endorse the project

Identify the Type of Project

- Documentation
- Improvement
- Renewal
- Standardization
- Development
- Maintenance

State Project Objectives

Objectives provide focus for the project. They keep the team members moving in the same direction. Objectives might include the following:

- Improve quality.
- Eliminate waste of time, energy, space, equipment, materials, and so on.
- Streamline.
- Discover/locate and correct causes of processing errors.
- Adapt processes to new requirements.
- Clarify procedures.
- Create clear, concise documentation.

Determine the Scope

Scope also provides focus for the project. It establishes parameters for the project and keeps the team members from straying into adjacent areas. It defines the following:

- The major systems and documents that support the process
- The start point
- The end point
- The work areas involved

Identify Team Members

- Team members should represent each of the work areas involved.
- Teams should be composed of knowledgeable, experienced veterans who actually do the work.
- Technical specialists should also serve as team members.
- Teams should elect a team leader and a recorder to document ideas and assignments.
- Five or six team members is a comfortable group size; beyond eight is difficult.
- Larger projects can be broken into subprojects with separate teams (team leaders meet to coordinate).

Announce the Project

- Call a meeting of all people from the areas that will be affected by the project (5 to 10 minutes, usually at the close of the work day, or at lunch in a large assembly area).
- The process owner should announce the project to all employees in the areas affected by the project.
- Emphasize the importance of the project.
- Emphasize management's commitment to the project.
- Relay management's expectation of contributions from top-notch employees.
- Encourage all employees to discuss ideas with the team member from their area.
- Introduce the team leader, the team recorder, the project facilitator, and the other team members.

- Things will change: Indicate that processes will change and will affect some jobs, and some jobs may be eliminated.
- Assure no loss of employment: Some jobs may go but people will not go—not as a result of any work improvement effort.

CAPTURE THE FACTS

- Observe knowledgeable employees doing the work at the workplace.
- Get facts primarily from observation interspersed with questions—people can usually show you faster than they can describe, and demonstration is much closer to reality than words.
- Don't trust detail to memory.
- Observe more than one work cycle and worker when applicable, but don't try to chart every variation.
- Don't look for faults.
- Represent the normal work cycle and major alternatives.
- Be methodical—follow and list steps in detailed order.
- Work quickly.
- Clarify uncertainties.
- Err on the side of too much information.
- Be accurate and legible so the data can be audited/reviewed.
- Once charted, walk the path again for verification.
- Stick to simply identifying steps and avoid detail of how steps are performed—this saves an enormous amount of time.
- Make sure people understand what you are doing and why they are involved.
- Respect work schedules and job-related interruptions.
- Assume the role of fact finder—the people are the experts.
- Collect the data quickly, using the symbols as shorthand.
  - Note *what* is done at each step.
  - Note *when* whenever there is a specific time (i.e., Monday at 9:00 a.m., at month end).
  - Note *when*—actually, "how long"—with delays, storage and other time-consuming steps.
  - Note the location *where* work is performed at the first step and every time the location changes—with each transportation step.

○ Note *who* every time a new person picks up the work.

○ Avoid getting into detail of *how* it is done.

○ Save *why* for analysis.

- Convert the notes to a chart the same day.

PREPARE AN AS-IS CHART

- Draw charts left to right.
- Begin every flow line with a label.
- Every action that occurs in a process can be represented by one of eight mutually exclusive, ASME symbols.
- Each symbol is described by an action verb.
- The Origination symbol shows the first time information is put on a document or entered in a file.
- The Add/Alter symbol shows all subsequent times that information is added to a document or changed.
- The Originate and Add/Alter symbols show ALL of the times that information changes in the process.
- The Do symbol shows any time a part is physically changed in a manufacturing process.
- The Handle symbol shows all occurrences of paper shuffling (sorting, stapling, separating, etc.) and keying through screens (accessing, searching, closing, saving, etc.), as well as make-ready and put-away in manufacturing processes.
- The Inspection symbol shows when a document is checked for quality or quantity.
- The Transportation symbol shows movement from one work area to another.
- The Delay/Storage symbol shows delays (generally, when the item will be processed further in the short term) and storage (usually at the end of a document line).
- The Destroy symbol shows when a document or product is discarded or when a file is deleted.
- Conventions are the links we use to connect the symbols.
- A horizontal line connects one symbol directly to the next.
- A period indicates the end of a document flow.
- A Stop/Start convention shows an interruption in the flow where activities are not charted.

- Alternatives (a Decision Point with multiple branches) are placed in a flow where two or more alternate paths are possible.
- A dotted line is used for an alternate path that represents a correction or rejection routine.
- A Rejoin shows two alternative flows (of the same item) joining back together.

Documents may interrelate several ways:

- An effect shows a source item affecting another item (causing its origination, adding information to it, checking it, or selecting it).
  - You can identify sources of information with effects from the source items.
  - An effect always points into a symbol located on the line of the affected document.
- An opening bracket shows items that were being processed together, being separated to be processed individually. When an item is separated or split into multiple items, the flow line splits into multiple lines.
- A closing bracket shows multiple process flows joined to be processed together. When multiple items are gathered and processed together, multiple flow lines are grouped into a single line.
- Connectors are used to show where the flow of a document continues on a different chart or elsewhere on the same chart (e.g., rework—when an item loops back to an earlier position in the flow—or with iterations of a process segment that is performed a number of times, such as in batch processing).

GET THE TEAM MEMBERS INVOLVED

- Lay the chart out in front of the team members and let them discover any obvious improvements.
- The facilitator draws the chart and is the first person to become familiar with the big picture. It is likely that some improvements will be obvious. It is imperative that the facilitator not snatch the credit for these obvious improvements.
- The facilitator who takes credit for obvious improvements is apt to appear to be stealing glory from the team, and this will cause the team to lose interest. Likewise, if the team members see the facilitator doing the improvement, they may assume that is the way the project is supposed to be done and will hold back from getting involved. If the team members hold back, the facilitator won't find the less obvious improvements. Finding them requires the experience of the team.
- When team members find obvious improvements, they experience instant success that builds their confidence—confidence needed for finding the less obvious improvements.

BUILD A LIBRARY OF PROCESS CHARTS

It is prudent business process management to build a library of charts. Having a charts library supports continuous improvement, but only if it is set up correctly:

- Organize chart files in folders.
- Place one person in charge of managing the library.
- Establish a schedule for chart review.
- Establish managers as owners of each process.
- Designate process workers to monitor process segments.
- Encourage process owners to sponsor improvement projects.

USE THE CHARTS

- Supply charts for improvement projects.
- Supply charts and explain them to people in new positions.
- Supply charts to auditors.
- Maintain and supply charts to satisfy regulatory, audit, or certification requirements.

11

CONCLUSION

Man can make System great; it isn't System which makes man great.

—Confucius

If we want to be better at what we do, we need to be the masters of our processes. Without rigorous method and good tools, that won't happen. It isn't enough to look at our processes in a cursory fashion. We need to *look at them in detail* and *understand the details*. When we don't understand the details, we miss inefficiencies, redundancies, and cumbersome, counterproductive, and even fraudulent activities. However, when our processes are transparent, these problems become obvious, and opportunities for correcting them are apparent.

We wouldn't consider building an automobile, an aircraft, a home, or an office building without the benefit of a blueprint. Business processes, by contrast, are often built on the fly. Then when problems surface, they are modified piecemeal. Before long, they evolve into convoluted, confused bureaucracy that nobody understands completely.

It is a challenge to understand a complicated, detailed process that flows through several workstations, passes through departmental boundaries, causes the origination and dissemination of dozens of forms, logs, and reports, and requires access and manipulation of data in multiple systems by many users. But, just as we have clearly established in the building of complex machines and buildings, we can master the complexity with drawings.

This book has explained a straightforward approach that many people have used to capture the detail of their processes and to master them. Detailed process charts show the big picture while allowing us to focus on the details. They give us fresh eyes—an opportunity to view the work from a different vantage point and to see how pieces fit together.

Many organizations are benefiting from the use of detailed process charts around the globe—but many more are not. We need to instill into our organizations the discipline to become masters of our processes and not slaves to them. Senior executives must support this effort, beginning with a commitment to treat their people as the resource they are and not an expense to be eliminated. Then they need to staff the chart-building effort with good people who are skilled at charting, have them build and maintain a chart library, and see that the charts are made available to people throughout the organization. This done, they can expect steadily increasing mastery among their people as they strive to make the organization as good as it can be.

INDEX